About This Resource

Why is this topic important?

People smart individuals have a wide array of skills to bring out the best in colleagues, customers, direct reports, and management. When people in an organization are people smart, they like their jobs better, increase their prospects for advancement, and contribute to organizational performance. When individuals at all levels of an organization are trained in the PeopleSmart program, clear, honest communication is abundant and interpersonal tensions are reduced. As a result, the total organization is more successful.

What can you achieve with this resource?

PeopleSmart is a training program where managers, supervisors, team leaders, and anyone else whose people skills are critical to the success of the organization gain:

- awareness of their interpersonal strengths and weaknesses
- inspiration to work on their interpersonal development
- strategies that are immediately useful to start

How is this resource organized?

This comprehensive interpersonal skills training program can be conducted in twelve hours, either as a two-day workshop or shorter sessions over a longer period of time. It contains ten modules, eight of which focus on a core interpersonal skill. The program features "active training" techniques in which lecturing is minimized and learning activity is maximized. Much of the program is based on examining and practicing skills applicable to the actual work experiences of the participants. The active training techniques used in this program are designed to increase participation, enliven learning, deepen retention, and encourage application.

About Pfeiffer

Pfeiffer serves the professional development and hands-on resource needs of training and human resource practitioners and gives them products to do their jobs better. We deliver proven ideas and solutions from experts in HR development and HR management, and we offer effective and customizable tools to improve workplace performance. From novice to seasoned professional, Pfeiffer is the source you can trust to make yourself and your organization more successful.

Essential Knowledge Pfeiffer produces insightful, practical, and comprehensive materials on topics that matter the most to training and HR professionals. Our Essential Knowledge resources translate the expertise of seasoned professionals into practical, how-to guidance on critical workplace issues and problems. These resources are supported by case studies, worksheets, and job aids and are frequently supplemented with CD-ROMs, websites, and other means of making the content easier to read, understand, and use.

Essential Tools Pfeiffer's Essential Tools resources save time and expense by offering proven, ready-to-use materials—including exercises, activities, games, instruments, and assessments—for use during a training or team-learning event. These resources are frequently offered in looseleaf or CD-ROM format to facilitate copying and customization of the material.

Pfeiffer also recognizes the remarkable power of new technologies in expanding the reach and effectiveness of training. While e-hype has often created whizbang solutions in search of a problem, we are dedicated to bringing convenience and enhancements to proven training solutions. All our e-tools comply with rigorous functionality standards. The most appropriate technology wrapped around essential content yields the perfect solution for today's on-the-go trainers and human resource professionals.

Pfeiffer
www.pfeiffer.com   *Essential resources for training and HR professionals*

PeopleSmart

FACILITATOR'S GUIDE

Mel Silberman

Freda Hansburg

Authors of People*Smart: Developing Your Interpersonal Intelligence*

A Wiley Imprint
www.pfeiffer.com

ISBN-10: 0-7879-7923-8
ISBN-13: 978-0-7879-7953-9
Acquiring Editor: Lisa Shannon
Director of Development: Kathleen Dolan Davies
Developmental Editor: Susan Rachmeler
Production Editor: Dawn Kilgore
Editor: Rebecca Taff
Manufacturing Supervisor: Becky Carreño
Editorial Assistant: Leota Higgins
Printed in the United States of America

Printing   10   9   8   7   6   5   4   3   2

CONTENTS

Introduction

PeopleSmart is a comprehensive interpersonal skills program, based on the book **People*Smart:* Developing Your Interpersonal Intelligence** (Mel Silberman with Freda Hansburg, 2000, Berrett-Koehler). Whether to supplement existing soft skills training or to serve as the foundation of a new training initiative, **PeopleSmart** is a program through which everyone whose people skills are critical to organizational success can gain:

- awareness of their interpersonal strengths and weaknesses
- inspiration to work on their interpersonal development
- strategies that are immediately useful to start

Potential participants may include organizational leaders, associates, or intact teams.

What skills are developed in PeopleSmart?

1. Understanding people
2. Expressing thoughts and feelings clearly
3. Speaking up when your needs are not being met
4. Exchanging feedback
5. Influencing how others think and act
6. Bringing conflicts to the surface and resolving them
7. Collaborating with others
8. Shifting gears when relationships are unproductive

How does PeopleSmart work?

The program includes twelve hours of active training designed to encourage participation, increase learning retention, and promote on-the-job application of the eight interpersonal skills above. The ten modules feature experiential exercises, self-assessments, video demonstrations, skill practice, and action planning.

Training activities are tailored to participants' own situations to maximize on-the-job skill application. Participants identify their key business relationships—managers, customers, coworkers, direct reports. Then they choose situations for each relationship that they want to improve, along with actions to try out on the job. They practice and experiment with approaches to fully develop and apply the essential **PeopleSmart** skills within those relationships. Follow-up coaching can be used to support participants' development.

The optimal number of participants for a **PeopleSmart** program is sixteen. Classes of this size promote teamwork and interaction, while allowing sufficient individual instruction and feedback. While larger classes are possible, they tend to diminish the facilitator's ability to coach participants in skill practice. The minimum suggested class size is six.

How is the Facilitator's Guide organized?

The Facilitator's Guide is a detailed instructor's manual for conducting **PeopleSmart.** It includes a CD with PowerPoint® slides and video clips; instructions for creating other required course materials appear in appendices. In some cases, optional props are suggested, which the instructor may elect to purchase (see "Materials" section for sources). The Facilitator's Guide is designed for use with the **PeopleSmart** Participant Workbook and the People Quotient (PQ) Scale. In addition, instructors may wish participants to receive a copy of the book, **People*Smart*.**

Each module in the Facilitator's Guide is broken into component activities, with time frames, materials, and instructional steps clearly delineated on the right-hand pages and visual reproductions of the relevant materials on the left-hand pages. This keeps the facilitator oriented to the flow and content of the program, without having to flip pages and juggle reference materials.

Materials

The following is a list of materials and supplies you and your participants will utilize during this workshop.

AV EQUIPMENT
☒ Personal Computer ☒ Projection System ☒ External Sound Hookup/Video

GENERAL SUPPLIES
☒ Markers ☒ Post-it® Notes ☒ Masking Tape
☒ Name Tents ☒ Push Pins ☒ Index Cards
☒ Blank Flip Pad ☒ Flip-Chart Stand

Ideal room set-up is a horseshoe shape with small tables for small group activities.

SLIDES/VIDEO
Please refer to the Facilitator's CD

PREPARED FLIP-CHART PAGES
- What's in It for Me? (Mod. 1)
- Benefits of Understanding (Mod. 2)
- Dealing with a Schmoozer (Mod. 3)
- How Many Squares? (Mod. 5)
- Images of Conflict (Mod. 7)
- Conflict Styles at Work (Mod. 7)
- Real-World Problem Solving (Mod. 8)
- Cross Out the Letters: BSAINXLEATNTEARS (Mod. 9)

PARTICIPANT MATERIALS/ HANDOUTS

Required Course Materials:
- Participant Workbook for each participant
- People Quotient (PQ Scale) for each participant
- Sample "butterfly" and colored paper (see Appendix A)
- Drawings A and B in folders (see Appendix B)
- Envelopes with Broken Squares (see Appendix C)

Optional Props*:
- $1,000,000 bills
- Toy microphones
- Candy for prizes
- Eyeglasses
- Director's clapboard
- Two oranges
- Banana
- Ball of yarn

*Two sources for the optional training props are orientaltrading.com and trainerswarehouse.com.

Course Timeflow (Twelve hours total)*

Module 1	Working PeopleSmart	60 minutes
Module 2	Understanding People	90 minutes
Module 3	Expressing Yourself Clearly	90 minutes
Module 4	Asserting Your Needs	60 minutes
Module 5	Exchanging Feedback	60 minutes
Module 6	Influencing Others	60 minutes
Module 7	Resolving Conflict	90 minutes
Module 8	Being a Team Player	90 minutes
Module 9	Shifting Gears	60 minutes
Module 10	PeopleSmart Day-by-Day	60 minutes

*The course may be taught in a variety of formats, including two intensive six-hour days, or either three four-hour or four three-hour days. In these instances, the order of the modules may need to be altered to fit the time constraints. Allowing time between sessions makes it possible for participants to do skill practice as "homework" between classes.

Advice to Facilitators

1. **PeopleSmart** is a comprehensive and challenging program, both to learn and to teach effectively. It is best taught by experienced facilitators with a background in soft skills training. The program also lends itself well to co-facilitation, in which skill demonstrations can be conducted by a training team. To prepare yourself to teach the program, read the book People*Smart* as background on the content and to obtain numerous examples of situations you can use within the workshop. Practice the skills described in the book so that you are comfortable and proficient modeling them in the moment when you teach, using situations participants may present.

2. If possible, have participants complete The People Quotient (PQ) Scale prior to the course. You may also have them do other advance preparation, particularly if time is an issue, such as having them identify situations or relationships in which they would like to improve their interpersonal effectiveness.

3. Determine the audience for the course, which may be leaders, associates, intact teams, or heterogeneous work groups. Also find out about prior training participants have experienced and frame the course accordingly (e.g., as a "refresher" or "enhancement").

4. Take advantage of several instances in the course in which the participant is asked to select *situations* (e.g., Workbook, pp. 18) in which they want to improve or *actions* (e.g., Workbook, p. 15) to try out on the job. Consider requiring participants to submit these selections to their manager or other appropriate person who will hold them accountable. *Customize* some or all of those pages that contain these situations and actions so that they reflect as closely as possible the work environment of the participants. You may also limit the application of the course to only some of the four groups (customers, colleagues, manager, direct reports) referenced in the course materials.

5. Although this facilitator's guide is very detailed and at times "scripted," do *not* try to memorize each detail and script. Try to find your own words and illustrate key points with your own examples and personal stories. In addition, alter the sequence of activities when you feel it would be helpful to you in a particular situation. Skip parts that don't add value for you or the group you are training or consume too much time.

6. During the training program, participants are encouraged to discuss work situations in which they may be experiencing difficulties with other people (managers, customers, coworkers, or direct reports). Request that all such conversations, both in small groups and across the entire class, be treated as confidential.

7. Skill practice is a vital part of **PeopleSmart.** Several role-playing formats are used in the course design, such as skits, participant-coached role plays demonstrated by the instructor, and simultaneous role playing in pairs. Feel free to adjust these formats to your needs and the resistance level of the participants. Consider adding value to the course by arranging for video feedback. One idea is to create video feedback teams of four people. Provide each team with a video camera

and monitor. Allow them to take turns taping each other during parts of the course when participants are practicing **PeopleSmart** skills.

8. **PeopleSmart** modules end with "experiments in change"—suggested activities participants can try out on the job. Decide in advance how you will motivate and support participants in undertaking these experiments (for instance, by being available to them as a mentor or coach).

9. Consider reordering the sequence of modules to best meet your participants' needs. For example, you may find it useful to do Module 9, Shifting Gears, before Module 8, Being a Team Player, or after Module 2, Understanding People.

10. The course is designed for an estimated twelve hours of training. Do not allow these time allotments to be the sole determination of how you conduct the course. Make adjustments that are in the best interests of your participants. Moreover, schedule the course so that participants do not tire and have the opportunity to reflect and practice what they have learned. Here are some additional suggestions that can help you avoid wasting time:

   - *Start on time.* This act sends a message to latecomers that you're serious. In the event that all of the participants are not yet in the room, begin the class, if you wish, with a discussion or filler activity for which complete attendance is not necessary.

   - *Give clear instructions.* Do not start an activity when participants are confused about what to do. If the directions are complicated, put them in writing.

   - *Prepare visual information ahead of time.* Don't write lecture points on flip charts or the blackboard while participants watch. Have it pre-recorded. Also, decide whether recording participant input is really necessary. If so, don't record the discussion verbatim. Use "headlines" to capture what participants are saying.

   - *Don't let discussions drag on and on.* Express the need to move on, but be sure in later discussion to call on those who did not have a chance to contribute previously. Or begin a discussion by stating a time limit and suggesting how many contributions time will permit.

   - *Obtain volunteers swiftly.* Don't wait endlessly for them to emerge from the class. You can recruit volunteers before the session begins.

11. Arrange the physical environment to maximize participation and involvement by using one of the following arrangements:

U Shape

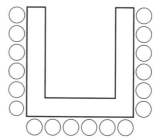

This is an all-purpose setup for up to eighteen participants (three sides of six). More participants will create a setup in which some are either too far from you or from each other. The participants have a reading and writing surface, can see you and visual media easily, and are in face-to-face contact with each other. It's also easy to pair participants, especially when there are two seats per table. The arrangement is ideal for distributing handouts quickly, since you can enter the U and walk to different points with materials. Be sure there is enough perimeter space so that subgroups of three or more can pull back from the tables and face each other.

Team Style

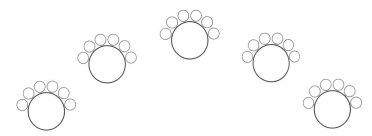

Grouping circular or oblong tables around the classroom enables you to promote team interaction. If you leave the mouth of each table empty, participants can easily see you in the front of the room without having to turn their chairs. The ideal team table seats six. You can then have a subgroup of six, two trios, or three pairs.

12. During group discussions, your role is to facilitate the flow of comments from participants. Although you need not interject after each person speaks, here are some ways to assist the group with their contributions:

   - *Paraphrase* what someone has said so that the participant feels understood and the other participants can hear a concise summary of what's been said at greater length.
   - *Check your understanding* against the words of a participant or ask a participant to clarify what he or she is saying.
   - *Compliment* an interesting or insightful comment.
   - *Elaborate* on a participant's contribution to the discussion with examples or suggest a new way to view the problem.
   - *Energize a discussion* by quickening the pace, using humor, or, if necessary, prodding the group for more contributions.
   - *Pull together ideas,* showing their relationship to each other.

13. When facilitating the experiential activities in **PeopleSmart,** here are some steps that will help you succeed:

   - *Explain your objectives.* Participants like to know what is going to happen and why.

- *Sell the benefits.* Explain why you are doing the activity and how it connects with previous activities.

- *Speak slowly and/or provide visual backup when giving directions.* Make sure the instructions are understandable.

- *Demonstrate the activity if the directions are complicated.* Let participants see it in action before they do it.

- *Divide participants into the subgroups before giving further directions.* If you don't, participants may forget the instructions while the groups are being formed.

- *Inform participants how much time they have.* State the time allotted for the entire activity and then announce periodically how much time remains.

14. Using active training techniques, like those built into the **PeopleSmart** design, tends to minimize the problem behaviors that often plague trainers who over-rely on lecture and full group discussion. Still, difficulties like monopolizing, distracting, and withdrawing may still occur. Here are some interventions you can use:

- *Signal nonverbally.* Make eye contact with or move closer to participants when they hold private conversations, start to fall asleep, or hide from participation. Press your fingers together (unobtrusively) to signal a wordy partici-pant to finish what he or she is saying. Make a "T" sign with your fingers to stop unwanted behavior.

- *Listen actively.* When participants monopolize discussion, go off on a tangent, or argue with you, interject with a summary of their views and then ask oth-ers to speak. Try acknowledging the value of their viewpoints or invite them to discuss their views with you during a break.

- *Get your ducks in order.* When the same participants speak up in class while others hold back, pose a question or problem and then ask how many peo-ple have a response to it. You should see new hands go up. Call on one of them. The same technique might work when trying to obtain volunteers for role playing.

- *Invoke participation rules.* From time to time, tell participants that you would like to use rules such as:
  - No laughing during role playing
  - Only participants who have not spoken as yet may participate
  - Build on one another's ideas
  - Speak for yourself, not for others

- *Use good-natured humor.* One way to deflect difficult behavior is to humor par-ticipants. Be careful, however, not to be sarcastic or patronizing. Gently protest the harassment (e.g., "Enough, enough for one day!"). Humorously put yourself down instead of the participant (e.g., "I guess I'm being stub-born, but . . . ").

- *Don't take personally the difficulties you encounter.* Remember that many problem behaviors have nothing to do with you. Instead, they are due to personal fears and needs or displaced anger toward someone else. See if you can pick up cues when this is the case and ask whether participants can put aside the conditions affecting their positive involvement in the training session.

Working PeopleSmart

Suggested Time: 60 minutes

PROP: *$1,000,000* bills (optional)

SLIDE #1: People Smart

SLIDE #2: How Many?

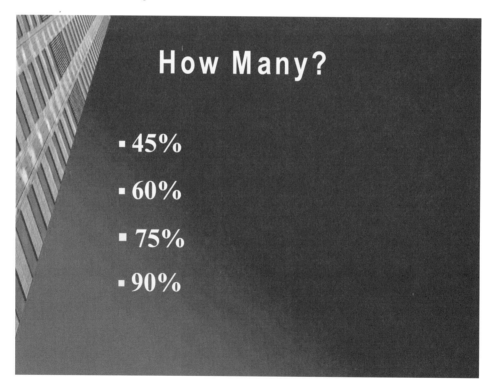

Opening Activity

Time: 5 minutes; *Materials:* $1,000,000 bills (optional); *References:* Slide #1, People*Smart,* Slide #2, How Many?

- **Show Slide #1:** People*Smart* as background display.
- **Say:** Before we formally get started, we are going to play "Who Wants to Be a Millionaire."
- **Show Slide #2:** How Many?
- **Instruct** participants to vote for the correct answer to the question "What percentage of firings stem from difficulties working with others?" Is it:

  45 percent

  60 percent

  75 percent

  90 percent
- **Say:** There will be two rounds of voting. In the first, I will ask for a show of hands so that you can use each other as a "lifeline" before casting your "final answer."
- **Conduct** first round of voting.
- **Say:** Now that you see what everyone else thinks, it's time for your *final answer.*
- **Conduct** second round of voting. This time, require participants to stand up for their final answer.
- **Tell** participants the correct answer is 90 percent* and, if available, distribute mock $1,000,000 bills to the winners. (One source is www.MillionDollarSource.com.)
- **Say:** This compelling statistic demonstrates how important interpersonal skills are to job success.

---

*Note:** This figure is from Marlene Lozada, "Social Misfits, Workplace Outcasts," *Vocational Educational Journal, 71,* 1996.

WORKBOOK, p. 1

Course Objectives

You will have the opportunity to . . .

- assess your skill levels for each of the eight PeopleSmart skills;
- select specific job-related situations in which you want to improve your skills;
- practice and apply three ways to develop each skill; and
- develop action plans to further practice each skill.

As a result of the course, you will come away with . . .

- greater awareness of your interpersonal strengths and weaknesses;
- inspiration to work on your interpersonal fitness; and
- immediately useful advice to get started.

1

WORKBOOK, p. 3

MODULE **1**

Working PeopleSmart

In this module, you will have the opportunity to . . .

- examine the components of working people smart

- discuss the benefits of working people smart

- analyze the four steps to developing interpersonal intelligence

- obtain a complete profile of your people smart skills

3

Review of Objectives

Time: 5 minutes: *References:* Workbook, pp. 1 & 3.

- **Refer to Workbook, p. 1:** Course Objectives.

- **Review** course objectives.

- **Say:** My pledge to you is that this course will not only ensure that you won't be fired because of insufficient people skills, but it will also increase your value to your organization. No twelve-hour training program can teach you everything. Imagine trying to play the piano well after only twelve hours of instruction. However, you will come away from this course with (1) incredible awareness of your interpersonal strengths and weaknesses, (2) several effective strategies you can implement right away, and (3) inspiration to develop yourself . . . on your own.

- **Refer to Workbook, p. 3:** Working PeopleSmart.

- **Review** Module 1 objectives.

- **Say:** Since you did pretty well on the "multiple choice" question a few minutes ago, let's see how you handle an "essay" question.

Toy Microphones (optional)

SLIDE #3: What Do These Three People Have in Common?

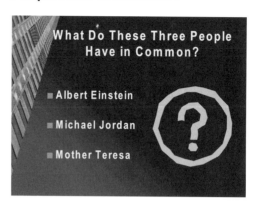

SLIDE #4: The 7 Intelligences

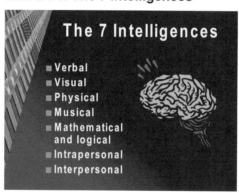

WORKBOOK P. 4

Different Kinds of Intelligence

Time: 15 minutes: *Materials:* Toy microphones (optional); *References:* Slide #3, What do these three people have in common? Slide #4, The Seven Intelligences; Workbook, p. 4.

- **Show Slide #3:** What Do These Three People Have in Common?

- **Ask** participants to share their responses. (*Use toy microphones, if available, to enhance discussion.*) Encourage several participants to participate by telling them that there is no one right answer to the question. Acknowledge their responses (e.g., they are all successful in their fields, all famous world-wide, all made a huge impact on the society, etc.). Compliment the quality and creativity that participants display. (A participant once quipped that they are all under 6 feet 7 inches! Another said: "They all could be played by Whoopi Goldberg.")

- **Show Slide #4:** The Seven Intelligences.

- **Say:** We can *also* say that all three of these people were or are "geniuses," but . . . in different ways. Albert Einstein excelled in visual, mathematical, and logical intelligence; Michael Jordan in physical intelligence, and Mother Teresa in interpersonal intelligence.

- **Refer to Workbook, p. 4:** Seven Intelligences.

- **Review** the kinds of intelligence. If you wish, attribute the concept of "multiple intelligences" to Howard Gardner of Harvard University. Indicate that Daniel Goleman's well-known book, *Emotional Intelligence,* focuses mainly on "intra" personal intelligence, which can be thought of as "self-smart." We will be focusing on "inter" personal intelligence or being "people smart."

- **Say:** Mother Teresa is a wonderful example of being people smart. Despite being a small, simple woman, she was able to empathize with the downtrodden and mobilize others to help them, a considerable feat when you think about the limited resources she had to work with.

- **Ask:** Who else would you call "people smart"? Invite responses, if any. You might mention presidents like Harry Truman and Ronald Reagan (two very different personalities, but both people smart). Rudy Giuliani might be a more recent example.

SLIDE #5: 4 Primary Relationships

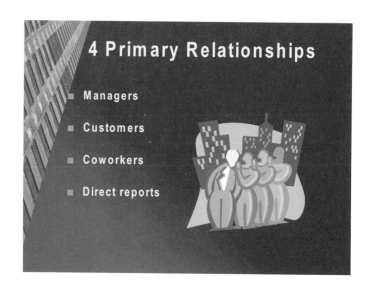

SLIDE #6: Why Work People Smart?

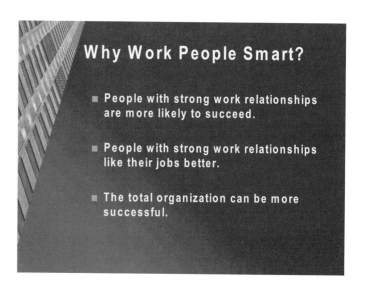

SLIDE #7: Individuals Who Are People Smart

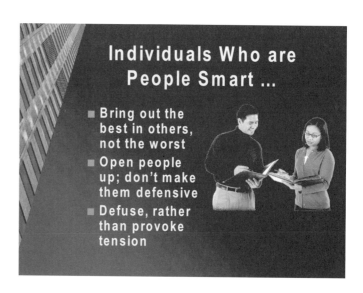

Introduction to Working PeopleSmart

Time: 10 minutes; *References:* Slide #5, Four Primary Relationships; Slide #6, Why Work People Smart?; Slide #7, Individuals Who Are People Smart.

- **Show Slide #5:** Four Primary Relationships.
- **Say:** None of us will be as people smart as Mother Teresa, but all of us are in the people business, even if our jobs are technical in nature. Here are four groups of people with whom we might have a work relationship in which it pays to be people smart: the person we report to, our peers/coworkers/teammates, our customers, and the people who report to us. We will refer to these relationships throughout the course. Here are three important reasons to invest in these relationships.
- **Show Slide #6:** Why Work People Smart?
- **Discuss** the three reasons: **(1) People with strong work relationships are more likely to advance in the organization.** As we said, an estimated 90 percent of firings are the result of poor people skills. If you lack technical knowledge, you can be trained or coached, or you can learn informally on the job. Poor people skills are a greater liability. However, they can be improved as well through training and coaching. If your people skills improve, you not only keep your job, but also increase your prospects for advancement. A recent survey of chief financial officers found that their top consideration in hiring senior level employees was their interpersonal skills [reported in *Training,* February 2002].

  (2) People with strong work relationships like their jobs better. Being good at what you do isn't enough if you can't enjoy working with the other people around you. More people complain about the people they work with than the work they have to do. Good working relationships make even the worst job bearable.
- **Ask:** Do you agree? **Point out** that a survey of 8,000 people in thirty-five industries found that among the top ten drivers that kept them in their jobs were relationships and a supportive boss [reported in *TD,* January 2002].

  (3) The total organization is more successful. A company's products and services are only as good as the people who create and provide them. When you and everyone else work effectively with others, the collaboration needed to drive organizational performance increases. Your customers are also pleased because they, too, appreciate how people skilled you are.
- **Say:** Being people smart is not *just* something we try to do with people we already have good relationships with. It's especially important when you are working with difficult people or having difficult conversations. Individuals who are people smart are gifted at bringing out the best in difficult people and circumstances.
- **Show Slide #7:** Individuals Who Are People Smart.
- **Say:** Working people smart means that you do what's in your power to have a better working relationship with others . . . despite their shortcomings. Individuals who are people smart open people up, rather than make them defensive, and defuse, rather than provoke tension.
- **Ask:** Do you know anyone you'd consider people smart? What makes you say that? **Discuss** one or two responses.

SLIDE #8: The 8 Essential PeopleSmart Skills

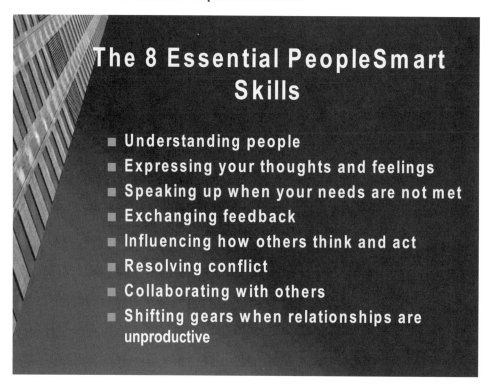

WORKBOOK p. 5

Working PeopleSmart   5

The Eight Essential PeopleSmart Skills

★ ★ ★

1. Understanding people

2. Expressing your thoughts and feelings clearly

3. Speaking up when your needs are not being met

4. Asking for feedback from others and giving them quality feedback in return

5. Influencing how others think and act

6. Bringing conflicts to the surface and resolving them

7. Collaborating with others, as opposed to doing things by yourself

8. Shifting gears when relationships are unproductive

The Eight PeopleSmart Skills

Time: 10 minutes; *Materials:* The PQ Scale; *References:* Slide #8, The Eight Essential PeopleSmart Skills; Workbook, p. 5.

- **Explain** that being people smart is a multi-faceted competence, not just a simple trait. It is a complex way of being intelligent that is just as important as how you master intellectual skills.

- **Say:** Here are the skills we consider to be the elements of being people smart.

- **Show Slide #8:** The Eight Essential PeopleSmart Skills.

- **Refer to Workbook, p. 5:** The Eight Essential PeopleSmart Skills.

- **Explain** that these are the eight essential PeopleSmart skills, which, together, make up your PeopleSmart Quotient, or PQ. We'll have the luxury of going into each skill in depth during the course.

- **Distribute** The PQ Scale to participants (if not already completed). [If ratings were completed prior to the course, ask participants to refer to their completed scales, and go to "pair participants," below.]

- **Say:** I'd like you to complete the PQ rating scale for yourself in your work role. Try to be as honest and objective as you can. You might ask yourself how your supervisor, coworkers, or customers see you.

- **Review** the rating scale and how to score it. Allow participants to complete their ratings.

- **Pair participants** with partners and invite them to compare their PQ ratings. Explain that they do not need to discuss specific scores, but rather the general trends of where their strengths and weaknesses lie. Allow time for the discussions; then reconvene the group.

- **Say:** However you scored, I hope this course will help you to improve your skills.

SLIDE #9: 3 Key Steps to Change

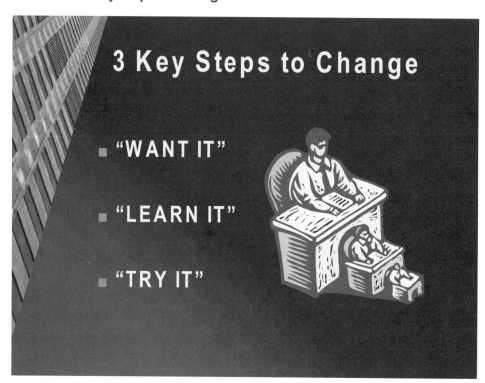

WORKBOOK p. 6

Three Key Steps to Change

★ ★ ★

You've got to "WANT IT"   1

You are more likely to be motivated if you are aware of when and where you need the skill the most. Choose a situation or two in which you want to excel.

You've got to "LEARN IT"   2

Become familiar with the skills possessed by people who exemplify each of the interpersonal intelligences.

You've got to "TRY IT"   3

Most people make the mistake of going for broke and then fizzle out when results don't come quickly. By offering you some "experiments in change," we'll help you test your wings and find the initial success to sustain yourself for further practice.

Three Steps to Change

Time: 5 minutes; *Materials:* Slide #9, Three Key Steps to Change; Workbook, p. 6.

- **Say:** Although we all have our areas of strength and weakness, interpersonal intelligence is not fixed. People can learn to become more adept at being people smart throughout their lives. However, it will take some hard work because adults don't change easily. Here is a little demonstration of that.

- **Instruct participants:** Fold your arms without thinking. Now fold them the opposite way so that you switch which arm is on top. Feel awkward? You bet. Well, stay that way for a minute. Now, if your legs are not already crossed, cross them without thinking about it. Now the upper part of your body is still uncomfortable, but your lower part is nice and comfortable. Cross your legs the opposite way. All of you is now out of your comfort zone. This is what it means for adults to change. We have to endure feeling uncomfortable and "wrong" for a while.

- **Show Slide #9:** Three Key Steps to Change.

- **Refer to Workbook, p. 6:** Three Key Steps to Change.

- **Explain:** In order to work a new behavior into your life, you need to do these three things.

  1. **You've got to "WANT IT."** From the start, be honest with yourself and determine whether you want to develop your PQ. You need to have specific goals in mind. You are more likely to be motivated if you are aware of when and where you need the skill the most. To help you make this connection, we will provide you with lists of situations in which you might find the skill in question to be particularly relevant in your job at the moment. Choose a situation or two in which you want to excel.

  2. **You've got to "LEARN IT."** Interpersonally intelligent people do certain things very well. Become familiar with the skills possessed by people who exemplify each of the eight components of PQ. While you don't need a whole course in each area to make some changes, it is important to acquire a few basics.

  3. **You've got to "TRY IT."** Most people make the mistake of going for broke and then fizzle out when results don't come quickly. With each aspect of interpersonal intelligence, we will encourage you to conduct an "experiment in change." We want you to try on a small change in behavior for size and see whether you like what happens. Don't kid yourself: you won't persist unless you find that there is something in it for you. By offering you some "experiments in change" for your consideration, we will help you to test your wings and find the initial success to sustain yourself for further practice.

- **Say:** The steps apply to any area of self-improvement. For example, suppose you wanted to quit smoking. Even if you admit to yourself that it's a bad habit, you still have to really *want* to do something about it, especially if you enjoy smoking. Therefore, it may prove necessary to keep in mind specific situations in which your smoking bothers you, such as when you jog and feel short of breath, or when you find yourself watching the clock in a meeting because you want a cigarette. Next you might find it helpful to *learn* about the latest methods for quitting, such as nicotine patches or "SmokeEnders" groups. When you decide to *try* something different, it will feel like an "experiment in change" to get through a day without a cigarette. If the experiment is successful, you may then be able to build the approach you have been using into your lifestyle.

- **Ask** participants for any examples of changes they tried, successfully or unsuccessfully, to make and discuss how the steps could apply.

- **Say:** Let's get going with the "want it" step right away.

Flip Chart: What's in it for Me?

WIFM
Customers:
Coworkers:
Manager:
Direct Reports:

WORKBOOK p. 7

Working PeopleSmart   7

WIFM (What's in it for me?)

★✦✱

For each of your primary relationships, first write the names of people who belong and
then select two situations in which you would like to improve your people skills.

My Customers _____

_____ Understanding customers' resistance to trying new products or services

_____ Convincing customers to hear me out

_____ Eliciting feedback from customers

_____ Figuring out customers' motivation

_____ (Other): _____

My Coworkers _____

_____ Reaching consensual decisions in team meetings

_____ Understanding a difficult coworker

_____ Drawing out the views of a coworker who's quiet or new

_____ Asserting my needs with coworkers

_____ (Other): _____

My Manager _____

_____ Giving feedback to my manager

_____ Negotiating work schedules with my manager

_____ Getting my point across to my manager

_____ Getting unstuck when I feel in a rut with my manager

_____ (Other): _____

My Direct Reports _____

_____ Giving clear instructions

_____ Seeking feedback from supervisees

_____ Motivating subordinates

_____ Getting conflicts out in the open

_____ (Other): _____

WIFM

Time: 10 minutes: *Materials:* Prepared flip chart: WIFM; *References:* Workbook, pp. 7.

- **Refer to Workbook, p. 7:** WIFM.

- **Say:** Did you know that everyone's favorite radio station is WIFM—What's in it for me? We'd like to know right from the beginning of this course in which situations you want things to go better for you.

- **Say:** Notice the lines after "My Customers," "My Coworkers," "My Manager," and "My Direct Reports." Write in the first names or initials of people who fit those categories in your work. Skip any category that does not apply to you.

- **Instruct** participants to look at the sample situations listed for each of their primary work relationships and to choose two situations for each relationship in which they'd like to focus on improving their interpersonal skills.

- **Chart** some of the situations chosen. Elicit some details for examples you can use as references throughout the course.

- **Summarize:** We have introduced the skills of working people smart, their importance, and the situations in which we can use them. We will now be looking at each of the skills in more depth and learning some of the secrets of people smart individuals.

Understanding People

Suggested Time: 90 minutes

PQ
Scale

SLIDE #10: Understanding People

SLIDE #11: "You can see a lot just by listening."

WORKBOOK p. 9

MODULE **2**

Understanding People

"You can see a lot just by listening."

—Yogi Berra

In this module, you will have the opportunity to . . .

- discuss the difference between labeling people and understanding them

- assess a person who is difficult to understand to discover what makes that person tick

- practice "listening for understanding" through interviewing

- learn three ways to interpret puzzling behavior

- select "experiments in change" at work

9

Introduction

Time: 5 minutes; *Materials:* PQ Scale; *References:* Slide #10, Understanding People, Slide #11, "You can see a lot . . .", Workbook, p. 9.

- **Show Slide #10:** Understanding People.

- **Refer to Workbook, p. 9:** Understanding People.

- **Explain** that figuring out what makes people tick is the most basic people smart skill.

- **Say:** With each new module, we will ask you to work with a new partner. When you move, bring your work materials with you. You will be sharing work-related situations with your partners and will need to keep what they share in this room in order to create a safe environment in the class.

- **Ask** participants to obtain a new partner and change seats, if necessary.

- **Show Slide #11:** "You can see a lot just by listening."

- **Say:** Yogi Berra was right that good listening is the start of understanding people. But to really get below the surface and read people effectively, there are some other skills involved, too.

- **Refer to Workbook, p. 9:** Understanding People.

- **Briefly review** module objectives.

- **Refer participants to PQ Scale:** Skill 1 and ask them to take a second look at their ratings for skill 1, identifying strengths and weaknesses.

- **Ask:** Which of the five skill behaviors do you find the most difficult?

- **Explain** that one of the problems we often have in understanding people is our tendency to write them off when their behavior doesn't make sense to us.

Flip Chart: Benefits of Understanding

SLIDE #12: Understanding Does Not Mean Acceptance

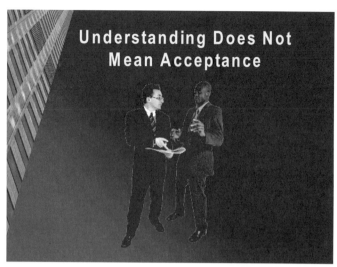

WORKBOOK p. 10

Interpreting Behavior

★★★

> Steve is arrogant, opinionated, and sloppy about his work . . . yet highly critical of others. He often makes crude or insensitive comments to people and reacts very defensively to any type of suggestion or criticism, no matter how constructive.
>
> Steve "stumbled" onto his job at our company. Despite the training he's received, the job is a little out of his league. He knows it. And he knows that everyone else knows it. Yet he gives off an air of superiority. He won't ask for help or advice. And if help or advice is offered, he rejects it.
>
> *I JUST DON'T GET HIM.*

Describe someone you "just don't get."

_____

_____

_____

_____

_____

_____

_____

_____

_____

_____

_____

_____

_____

_____

_____

Understanding a Difficult Person

Time: 15 minutes; *Materials:* Flip chart, Benefits of Understanding; *References:* Slide #12, Understanding Does Not Mean Acceptance; Workbook, p. 10.

- **Refer to Workbook, p. 10:** Interpreting Behavior.
- **Explain** that "Steve" is a hypothetical case in point. Ask them to notice how Steve's coworker describes him.
- **Recruit** a volunteer to read the description of Steve aloud to participants.
- **Instruct** participants to describe the behavior of someone from their work situation whom they just don't get. Explain that this could be someone who's too quiet and hard to read, or perhaps a manager who's much more formal than most people in their organization. Ask them to write the specific behaviors of the person that puzzle them on the workbook page, ending with "I just don't get him/her."
- **Say:** The first problem we have when we don't "get" someone is that we often start to label him or her. We put the person "in a box," just like Steve's coworker did. But that doesn't help.
- **Ask:** How did Steve's coworker label him?
- **Discuss** responses.
- **Say:** We may be most likely to label people when we are out of our comfort zones. This can happen when they are very different from us in values, style, and preferences. We keep our distance and reconfirm our labels. Sometimes the labeling occurs because the other person is like us in ways we would hate to admit to ourselves. Often we even go beyond labeling to attributing motives that have no basis in fact. When we misinterpret or distort who the person is, it doesn't help us understand him or her. Labeling may supply us with a lot of "what," but no "why." We need to challenge ourselves to be *curious,* not *furious* with people who make us uncomfortable.
- **Instruct** participants: Go back and re-read your own descriptions of your difficult person. Did you label him or her?
- **Say:** Someone who is people smart tries to develop an "empathic understanding" of a person whose behavior is puzzling. The people smart person may not like or accept the other person's behavior, but nonetheless explores why the person acts in the ways he or she does.
- **Show Slide #12:** Understanding Does Not Mean Acceptance
- **Say:** We can try walking in another person's shoes, without agreeing with his views or tolerating irresponsible behavior.
- **Ask:** What's the benefit of trying to understand a difficult person?
- **Chart** responses. If not stated, make the point that understanding can unlock new ways to relate to the person that will be more productive for both of you. You may gain a new perspective on the person, and it may help you get some distance and avoid taking what the person does too personally. Sometimes, the other person simply appreciates your attempts to understand him or her, and that act brings on a positive change.
- **Ask:** Can you share any examples of this from your own experiences?
- **Ask:** So how do we go about understanding someone? Let's look at the next slide.

SLIDE #13: 5 Ways to Understand People

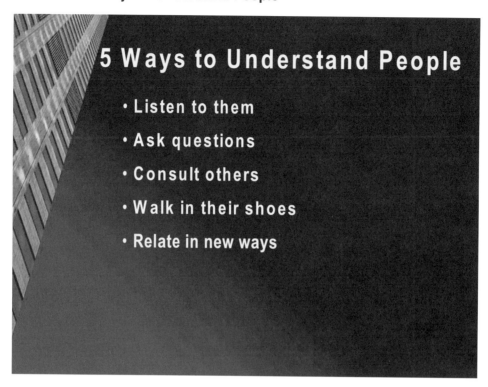

WORKBOOK p. 11

Understanding People   11

Five Ways to Understand People

★✦★

Which of the below have you done with regard to
your difficult person?

_____ 1. Take time to listen.

_____ 2. Ask questions about his or her thoughts
        and feelings.

_____ 3. Consult other people who may have
        insights about this person.

_____ 4. Try "walking in his or her shoes" by
        looking at events from this person's
        point of view.

_____ 5. Relate to the person in new ways.

Five Ways to Understand

Time: 15 minutes; *References:* Slide #13, Five Ways to Understand People; Workbook, p. 11.

- **Show Slide #13:** Five Ways to Understand People.

- **Discuss** the five ways. Point out that actively listening involves paraphrasing, clarifying, and acknowledging the person's feelings as you listen to him or her. Asking probing questions means drawing the person out, but not interrogating. Consulting others involves getting input from people who can help you understand the person, not just commiserate with you about how difficult the person is. Walking in another person's shoes requires you to put your own preconceptions aside and look through the other person's eyes. Relating in new ways means being willing to experiment with a different approach.

- **Refer to Workbook, p. 11:** Five Ways to Understand People.

- **Ask:** Which of these steps have you taken to understand the person you described on page 10 of your workbook? (Give participants a few minutes to review the list.)

- **Say:** Let's focus first on listening as a way to understand a difficult person. When it comes to "active" listening, we can understand people by using a range of actions. In some cases, it may be useful to spend more time hearing the person out, just by listening attentively and focusing on what is being said, without much interpretation or intrusion. If you want to ask a question, you use a gentle touch. We call this *"focusing."*

- **Say:** In other cases, another approach may prove useful. Here, you might be asking the person some direct questions about himself or herself. In this mode, you are *interviewing* more than *focusing.*

WORKBOOK p. 12

Interviewing

Directions

Interview your partner about his or her Difficult Person.

- Ask questions and dig for deeper understanding.

- Solicit your partner's viewpoint (but hold back on your own).

- Seek clarification and illuminate the feelings behind what your partner is saying.

- Obtain information that hasn't been stated.

Debrief

- How did the interview go? What was challenging?

- What benefits did you and your partner experience by interviewing him or her?

Interviewing for Understanding

Time: 20 minutes; *References:* Workbook, p. 12.

- **Refer to Workbook, p. 12:** Interviewing.

- **Tell** them that they will now have the opportunity to practice this form of active listening.

- **Say:** This will be an opportunity to do two things: (1) to practice tuning in through interviewing and (2) to talk with their partners about their difficult person in order to begin getting to the "why" of his or her puzzling behavior . . . to go from being "furious" to being "curious."

- **Review** the directions for interviewing:

    1. Ask questions and dig for deeper understanding.

    2. Solicit your partner's viewpoint (but hold back on your own).

    3. Seek clarification and illuminate the feelings behind what your partner is saying.

    4. Obtain information that hasn't been stated.

- **Demonstrate** interviewing with a volunteer. Have the volunteer describe his or her difficult person and show the steps of interviewing. At some point during the interview, suddenly begin giving your own opinion. Quickly stop yourself.

- **Say:** Now, what did I just do? If no one answers correctly, say: I just gave my opinion. This is just what you *shouldn't* do when interviewing.

- **Instruct** participants to pair and take turns interviewing their partner as he or she describes his/her difficult person. Suggest that the speaker begin with a brief account of the difficulties he or she has experienced with the difficult person. Then allow the interviewer to start asking questions. [*If time is limited, have only one round in which one person interviews.*]

- **Debrief** in the large group, asking participants to identify the benefits they and their partners received by interviewing each other.

- **Say:** Now, let's look at another of the five ways to understand.

SLIDE #14: How Do We Compare with Others?

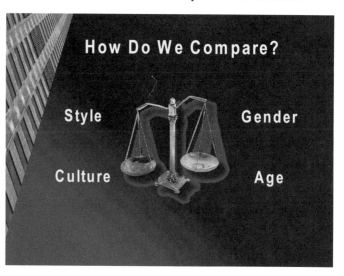

WORKBOOK p. 13

Understanding People   13

How Do We Compare with Others?

★★★

Because of differences in style, gender, age, and culture, we might be very different in the following ways. *Circle* the point on each relevant continuum that fits the way you see your difficult person. Put a *square* on the point that fits the way you see yourself.

Spontaneous . . . . Careful
    *   *   *   *   *

Social . . . . Private
    *   *   *   *   *

Emotional . . . . Analytic
    *   *   *   *   *

"Take charge" . . . . Responsive
    *   *   *   *   *

Competitive . . . . Collaborative
    *   *   *   *   *

Give opinions . . . . Ask questions
    *   *   *   *   *

Intense . . . . Easygoing
    *   *   *   *   *

Focused . . . . Multitasking
    *   *   *   *   *

Confronting . . . . Avoiding
    *   *   *   *   *

Self-oriented . . . . Group-oriented
    *   *   *   *   *

Respect for talent . . . . Respect for authority
    *   *   *   *   *

Loose . . . . Rule-oriented
    *   *   *   *   *

How Do We Compare?

Time: 15 minutes; *Materials:* Pair of rosy sunglasses and darker pair (optional); *References:* Slide #14, How Do We Compare with Others?; Workbook, p. 13.

- **Say:** One of the obstacles to understanding others is the fact that we all see the world through our own lenses.

- **Put on** a pair of rosy sunglasses (optional).

- **Say:** Some of us may see things though rosy glasses, in mostly positive terms, while others wear darker lenses and see things more negatively.

- **Change** optional glasses to a darker pair.

- **Say:** The more we can recognize the glasses others are looking through, the better we can understand their perspectives and behavior.

- **Show Slide #14:** How Do We Compare with Others?

- **Say:** The "glasses" through which people see the world are often related to areas such as personal style, gender, age, and cultural background. Making the effort to consider factors like these can help us understand others. Let's try this with your difficult person.

- **Refer to Workbook, p. 13:** How Do We Compare with Others?

- **Instruct** them to identify on which of the dimensions they have differences and similarities with their difficult person. Have them circle the point on each continuum that fits the way they see their difficult person and put a square on the point that fits the way they see themselves.

- **Instruct** participants to discuss their comparisons with their partners.

- **Debrief** by asking if anyone would like to share any insights from their discussion with his or her partner. Or survey the groups to see which differences were most illuminating for them. Note that sometimes a person we find to be difficult is similar to us, rather than different from us. Sometimes, we are upset by things about another person that are also upsetting aspects of ourselves.

- **Say:** Now let's see how we can go to yet another level of understanding people.

WORKBOOK p. 10

Interpreting Behavior

⋆✦★

> Steve is arrogant, opinionated, and sloppy about his work . . . yet highly critical of others. He often makes crude or insensitive comments to people and reacts very defensively to any type of suggestion or criticism, no matter how constructive.
>
> Steve "stumbled" onto his job at our company. Despite the training he's received, the job is a little out of his league. He knows it. And he knows that everyone else knows it. Yet he gives off an air of superiority. He won't ask for help or advice. And if help or advice is offered, he rejects it.
>
> *I JUST DON'T GET HIM.*

Describe someone you "just don't get."

_____

_____

_____

_____

_____

_____

_____

_____

_____

_____

_____

_____

_____

_____

SLIDE #15: The 3 C's

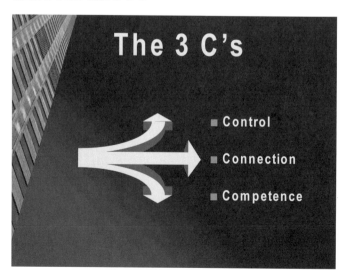

The 3 C's

Time: 15 minutes; *References:* Slide #15, The 3 C's; Workbook, pp. 10, 14, 15.

- **Refer** participants back to the description of Steve on Workbook page 10: Interpreting Behavior.

- **Ask:** Why might Steve be behaving that way?

- **Discuss** participants' interpretations. Don't allow labeling. Try to get participants to look at the possible motives behind Steve's behavior.

- **Explain:** We are not suggesting that you take a graduate course in psychology, but we want to give you some ideas about looking below the surface to understand people. You don't have to become Sigmund Freud, but it's people smart to try to gain some psychological understanding of people. When we understand people's motives, we can often deal with them more comfortably and effectively.

- **Say:** There are countless frameworks for analyzing people, but here is one simple and helpful way to look below the surface.

- **Show Slide #15:** The 3 C's.

- **Explain** each of the C's as basic human needs:

  Control is about having power over your life, being in the driver's seat instead of the passenger seat.

  Connection is our need for inclusion, support, love, and acceptance

  Competence is our need for success, demonstrating mastery, and being recognized for doing so.

- **Explain:** At any given time, we may be overly anxious about obtaining one or more of these goals and, as a result, behave in some extreme ways. For example, someone who is anxious about control might act like a "control freak," who needs everything done his or her way. In contrast, someone else who is anxious about control may typically want others to call the shots. We may handle these anxieties differently in different contexts. For instance, a manager might be very concerned with demonstrating competence at work but much more concerned with connection at home. You also need to be aware of your own 3 C's. We can misread people when we look at them through our glasses instead of recognizing theirs. For example, we might interpret a manager as "controlling" if she hovers around us or asks us too many questions about ourselves or our work, but she might actually be trying to "connect" with us.

- **Ask** participants how they might apply the 3 C's to Steve. Discuss answers and, as needed, make the points that Steve may use his arrogance to push people away and avoid connection because he's afraid others will reject him. Or he may be very insecure about his competence and thinks that he's safer if he keeps people at a distance. If we can understand Steve's motives, we may be able to relate to him better. For instance, if we know he's insecure about his competence, we could ask him for feedback about something instead of offering him feedback about his work.

WORKBOOK p. 14

Three Basic Needs

⋆✦ ✦

CONTROL
Having power over your life

CONNECTION
Inclusion, support, love

COMPETENCE
Succeeding, demonstrating mastery

How anxious is your own Difficult Person about meeting these needs?

Check any of the anxious behaviors he or she tends to exhibit:

Control
❏ Micromanages others
❏ Acts helpless and dependent
❏ Has great difficulty being flexible

Connection
❏ Rejects others
❏ Tries too hard to be accepted
❏ Seeks a lot of attention

Competence
❏ Brags a lot
❏ Puts him/herself down
❏ Easily becomes defensive

WORKBOOK p. 15

Working the Three C's

⋆✦ ✦

Below are some strategies that may help alleviate people's anxieties about **control, connection,** and **competence.** Check any that you think might be helpful to try with your difficult person.

Control
❏ Keep the person informed and up-to-date.
❏ Offer choices and decisions.
❏ Ask: "What role do you want (in this project)?"

Connection
❏ Show the person attention before he or she seeks it.
❏ Tactfully and directly set limits when he or she demands too much attention.
❏ Offer greetings or conversation in small doses.

Competence
❏ Give genuine positive feedback proactively.
❏ Don't put the person on the spot in front of others.
❏ Give the person a task you know he or she can do successfully.

- **Say:** Now let's apply this to your own difficult person.

- **Refer to Workbook, p. 14:** Three Basic Needs.

- **Instruct** them to use the checklist to identify anxious behaviors their difficult person may be exhibiting. Invite them to share their interpretations with their partners.

- **Refer to Workbook, p. 15:** Working the 3C's.

- **Instruct** them to review the strategies and choose at least one that might be helpful with their Difficult Person. Invite them to share their choices with their partners.

- **Debrief** in the large group by asking whether anyone uncovered something potentially useful about his or her difficult person. Invite one or two participants to share examples.

WORKBOOK p. 16

TRY IT: Experiments in Change

⋆★✦

Select one of the following experiments. . . .

Improving Listening:

☐

Think of the person you consider the best listener you know, someone you invariably feel comfortable talking with. For a week, study his or her nonverbal behavior during conversations the person has with you or others. What does the person do that conveys interest and acceptance? Write down some of the behaviors you notice the person using. Next, notice whether any of these behaviors are part of your own present repertoire. If not, which of the behaviors would you be willing to try out? Choose one or two and practice them.

Decreasing Interruptions:

☐

For a couple of days, keep a log of your conversations at work and record how often you interrupt others. You can do this informally by placing an object, such as a coin or paperclip, in a particular pocket each time you catch yourself interrupting. Calculate the percentage of your conversations that included interruptions. How do you feel about your interruption rate? If you're unhappy with it, choose a specific person or situation and, for one full day, do not interrupt at all. Notice how this makes you feel and how others respond. See whether you can identify what makes it hard for you to hear people out.

Analyzing Goals:

☐

Think of someone you simply don't understand at all. Think about this person's behavior in a few key situations. What seems to be his or her primary goal: control, connection, or competence? Is this person's goal different from yours? When you recognize his or her usual goal, do you understand the person better? Would you change any of your own behavior in dealing with this person in the future?

Understanding Differences:

☐

Identify someone at work who's as different as possible from you. On a 1 to 10 scale, where 1 is the lowest and 10 the highest rating, rate how well you understand this person's values, assumptions, and motivation. Now list some of the ways this person is different from you, including goals, personal style, and demographic factors. Which of these differences may be interfering with your ability to understand this person? Try to imagine yourself as this person, seeing the world through his or her eyes. How do you feel? How do things seem different to you? Now re-rate your understanding of the person. Is there a change?

Closing

Time: 5 minutes; *References:* Workbook, p. 16.

- **Refer to Workbook, p. 16:** TRY IT: Experiments in Change.

- **Re-explain** the rationale for conducting an "experiment in change"—that unless we test the waters and see the results, we're unlikely to making lasting changes.

- **Encourage** them to select an experiment they are willing to try in the next week or so. [**Note:** if there will be some time between sessions, encourage participants to do one of the experiments before the group reconvenes.]

- **Summarize:** We've been looking at some of the ways that we can be people smart about understanding others. The flip side of understanding is getting others to understand *you*. In the next module, we will focus on how to convey our own thoughts and feelings in a people smart way.

Expressing Yourself Clearly

Suggested Time: 90 minutes.

SLIDE #16: Expressing Yourself Clearly

SLIDE #17: "Nothing is so simple that it cannot be misunderstood."

WORKBOOK p. 17

MODULE **3**

Expressing Yourself Clearly

"Nothing is so simple that it cannot be misunderstood."

—Jr. Teague

In this module, you will have the opportunity to . . .

- experience when words can be confusing to others

- assess your communication skills

- identify work situations in which clear communication is essential

- practice communicating about complex subject matter

- examine the concept of "owning your communication"

- select "experiments in change" at work

17

Introduction

Time: 10 minutes; *References:* Slide #16, Expressing Yourself Clearly, Slide #17, "Nothing is so simple . . ."; Workbook, p. 17.

- **Show Slide #16:** Expressing Yourself Clearly.

- **Say:** The second people smart skill is expressing yourself clearly.

- **Show Slide #17:** "Nothing is so simple that it cannot be misunderstood."

- **Say:** As technology gives us more and more ways to communicate, it also means we have more and more ways to be misunderstood. Words can be confusing, and here is a simple example.

- **Say:** Let me *run* this by you. When I leave here, I have to *run* off to my softball team practice. I hope when it's my turn to bat that I hit a *homerun.* Then I'll have to *run* around the bases. You know, we wear those old-fashioned uniforms, with stockings. Last week I had a *run* in mine. But still, our team is having quite a *run* of luck this season. Well, I guess I'm *running on* too much about the word *run.* [**Note:** You may use variations on this example. Women may prefer to say "I was *running* late this morning, tripped and got a *run* in my stocking. I thought I'd *run* into the pharmacy for another pair, but they had *run* out of my size. That's the kind of *run* of bad luck I've been having lately. No wonder I feel so *run* down!"]

- **Say:** Look at all the possible meanings in one three-letter word. Speaking or writing to others about virtually anything can involve the same confusion. Of the eight hundred words we tend to use daily, there are estimated to be 14,000 meanings. Something may be clear to us, but not to someone else, if all we rely on are the words we use. For instance, if I asked you to "put your things away," what would I mean?

- **Poll** the group for possible responses (e.g., your books, your coat).

- **Say:** Some of the things we say and hear all the time may be completely confusing to someone coming from a different environment. A foreigner might be thoroughly confused when he goes into an American supermarket and the cashier says: "Paper or plastic?" He may think the cashier wants to know if he is paying with cash or a credit card!

- **Say:** So here are our objectives for this module.

- **Refer to Workbook, p. 17**: Expressing Yourself Clearly.

- **Review** module objectives.

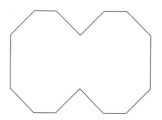

WORKBOOK p. 18

Getting Invested

⋆★✦

Two situations in which I want to improve my communication skills are . . .

❑ giving a presentation to clients on a complicated project

❑ orienting a new employee to office procedures

❑ presenting my ideas for improving an unsuccessful project to skeptical team members

❑ giving detailed instructions to a coworker

❑ conducting a performance review with a subordinate who doesn't recognize his/her work deficiencies

❑ updating my boss on the status of my projects

❑ conversing with important clients over a business lunch

❑ getting my point across to colleagues during meetings

❑ presenting my experience and qualifications during a job interview

❑ other: _____

Make a Butterfly

Time: 15 minutes; *Materials:* sample "butterfly" (see Appendix A) and colored paper, PQ Scale; *References:* Workbook, p. 18.

- **Say:** Communication also breaks down when we don't fully explain ourselves, expecting others to be mind readers. Here is an example.

- **Give** participants a blank sheet of colored paper.

- **Show** participants a sample "butterfly" created from a similar sheet of paper.

- **Say:** I'd like you to make a butterfly of your own by folding and tearing your paper correctly. Pay attention to me, because I'm only going to give these instructions once, without taking any questions. (Be firm about answering questions.)

- **Instruct** participants:

  Fold your paper in half.

  Tear off the upper right hand corner.

  Fold your paper in half again.

  Tear off the upper left hand corner.

  Fold your paper in half again.

  Tear off the lower right hand corner.

- **Ask** participants to hold up their "butterflies." The results will vary widely with few, if any, butterflies.

- **Say:** What's the matter? Can't you people follow directions? Why such poor results?

- **Acknowledge** participants' complaints that your directions were ambiguous. Explain that there were different ways to hold the paper, horizontally or vertically, from the start, and it wasn't clear which way to turn your paper. You needed to be a "mind reader" in order to do this correctly.

- **Refer participants to PQ Scale:** PeopleSmart Skill 2.

- **Instruct** them to review their skill ratings for PeopleSmart Skill 2.

- **Instruct** participants to rotate to a new partner.

- **Refer to Workbook, p. 18:** Getting Invested.

- **Tell** participants to select two situations from the list in which they want to improve their communication skills and then discuss them with their new partners.

- **Say:** Communication can become especially difficult when we try to convey something complicated. Next we'll do another exercise that illustrates these perils.

Drawing A

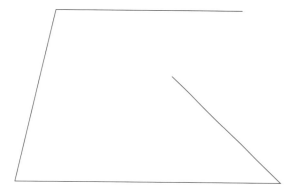

Drawing B

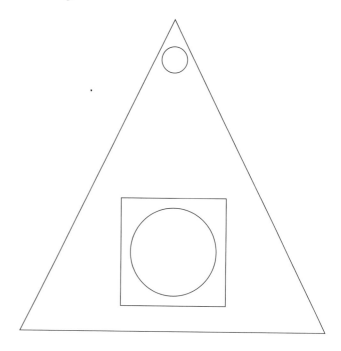

WORKBOOK p. 19

Expressing Yourself Clearly   19

Communicating When Things Are Complicated

★★★

Directions

- The Communicator and Receiver should sit back-to-back.

- The Receiver should not see the drawing!

- The Communicator is to describe the drawing to the Receiver so that the Receiver is able to draw it accurately.

- The Receiver may not ask questions.

- When finished, compare drawings.

- The Receiver should give feedback to the Communicator about what he or she did that was helpful or unhelpful.

Debrief

What can the Communicator do to be effective in this exercise?

Communicating Something Complicated

Time: 15 minutes; *Materials:* drawings A & B in folders (see Appendix B); *References:* Workbook, p. 19.

- **Designate** one person in each pair as the "communicator" and the other person as the "receiver."

- **Instruct** the pairs to sit back-to-back. Give each communicator a copy of Drawing A, stapled inside a folder so that no one else in the room can see the drawing. Give receivers a blank piece of paper and a pen or pencil.

- **Review the directions.** Ask the communicator to describe the drawing to the receiver so that the receiver is able to draw it accurately. *Forbid the receiver from asking questions of the communicator. Do not specify whether the communicators may ask the receivers questions (they may).*

- **Instruct** participants to compare the original drawing to the one made by the receiver when the receiver has finished drawing.

- **Tell** the receiver to give feedback to the communicator as to what he or she did that was helpful or unhelpful. [**Note:** if time is sufficient, you may do a second round in which the roles switch. Use Drawing B for Round 2 and provide a blank piece of paper for each receiver. Be sure that feedback is given in each round.]

- **Point out** that communication is a two-way process, and not a matter of talking one-way. In particular, in this exercise, the onus is on the communicator to ask the receiver questions such as: *"So far, so good?" "Was I clear?" "What's your understanding of what an equilateral triangle is?"* The task in this exercise is analogous to any situation in which something complicated has to be explained to someone else.

- **Refer to Workbook, p. 19:** Communicating When Things Are Complicated.

- **Debrief** with the question on the bottom of the page: "What can the Communicator do to be effective in this situation?"

- **Discuss** responses.

- **Say:** We could also say that to be effective, you must include the listener.

Toy Microphone
(optional)

SLIDE #18: 5 Steps to Include the Listener

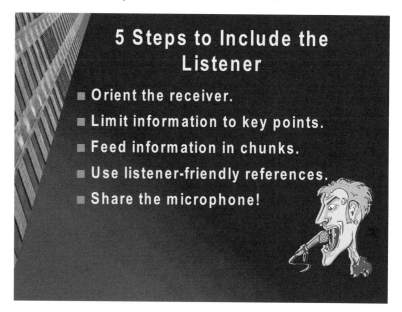

WORKBOOK p. 20

> 20   *PeopleSmart: Participant Workbook*
>
> Five Steps to Include the Listener
>
>
>
> 1. Orient the receiver.
> 2. Limit information to key points.
> 3. Feed information in chunks.
> 4. Use listener-friendly references.
> 5. Share the microphone.
>
> **Directions**
> Take turns explaining one of the following topics to your partner. Choose a topic about which you have some knowledge, but your partner does not.
>
> - The benefits of a product or service (e.g., a new drug,)
> - The features of a product or service (e.g., new operating system)
> - How to _____ (e.g., a safety procedure, an activity).
> - The difference between a _____ and a _____ (e.g., HMO/PPO, a PC and a MAC).
> - Tips for _____ (e.g., searching the web)
> - (Supply your own) _____
>
> **Debrief**
> 1. Give your partner feedback, referring to the list of tips above.
> 2. Agree on how to improve your presentations.

Including the Listener

Time: 25 minutes: *Materials:* toy microphone (optional); *References:* Slide #18, Five Steps to Include the Listener; Workbook, p. 20.

- **Show Slide #18:** Five Steps to Include the Listener.

- **Review** the tips, tying into participants' previous suggestions and pointing out any they overlooked. Emphasize that the communicator's job is not only to get the information across effectively but to include the receiver by "giving up the microphone."

- **Say:** (holding the toy microphone, if available) One of the most important things we can do to be clear is to stop talking and check in with the listener, instead of going on and on trying to make our point. By "giving the microphone to the listener," we give him or her a chance to ask questions or paraphrase what is heard. What reactions do you have to what I'm saying? (Hand the microphone to any participants who wish to respond.)

- **Refer to Workbook, p. 20:** Five Steps to Include the Listener.

- **Demonstrate** the tips given at the top of the page by explaining any technical topic about which you are knowledgeable with a volunteer participant who doesn't know much about the topic. When you are finished, **ask** participants whether you followed the guidelines.

- **Instruct** participants to pair with their partners and each to choose one of the complicated topics from the list (or supply one of their own) with which they are familiar and their partner is not. Ask them to take turns explaining their topics to each other, then to debrief together following the steps in the workbook. [*If time is limited, have each pair select only one person to do the activity. If you did only one round in the previous activity, have the person who was the receiver be the communicator this time.*]

- **Tell** participants to give the communicators feedback after their explanations, using the list of tips on the workbook page as a checklist, then agree on how to improve their presentations.

- **Invite** two volunteers to report the effective use of the guidelines by their own partner.

DEALING WITH A
SCHMOOZER

SLIDE #19: Straightforward Communication

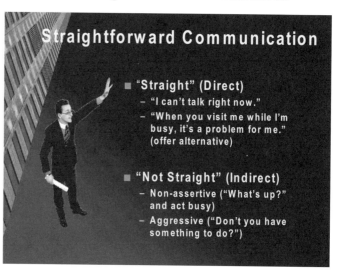

SLIDE #20: Barriers to Speaking Your Mind

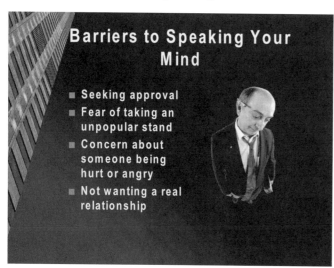

Being Straightforward

Time: 20 minutes; *Materials:* Prepared flip chart: Dealing with a Schmoozer; *References:* Slide #19, Straightforward Communication, Slide #20, Barriers to Speaking Your Mind; Workbook, p. 21.

- **Say:** We've been looking at situations in which our communication has centered on expressing complicated "facts" in a clear way. Let's look at something different. Imagine that you have been upset about an overly friendly coworker (a "schmoozer") who hangs around you a lot, telling you about matters that are not work-related, and doesn't give you enough privacy or time to get your work done. Sometimes you get rid of the "schmoozer" with some excuse, but he doesn't pick up on your hints. You realize that the time has come to address the problem. How might you deal with this situation? What exactly would you say?

- **Record** on the flip chart the suggestions you receive into two categories: direct and indirect, but do not reveal the names of the two categories at this point.

  Be sure to list any suggestions that involve hinting or hedging in the "indirect" column. Do the same with suggestions that ridicule, embarrass, or in any way label the coworker negatively as long as they do not state directly what the speaker thinks, feels, or wants.

  Only put suggestions in the "direct" column in which the speaker "owns" what he or she is saying, such as "I have a problem. When you come to visit me, I enjoy our conversations, but I get behind in my work. It would help me if we spent far less time together 'shooting the breeze.'"

- **Ask** participants what they think the two columns reflect.

- **Show Slide #19:** Straightforward Communication.

- **Ask** pairs to discuss its contents by themselves.

- **Say:** Sometimes we go through the front door with our thoughts and feelings, which is direct, and sometimes through the back door, which is indirect. Hostile remarks, such as "You're getting to be ruthless," are just as indirect as hints such as "I guess I'm overly sensitive." The bottom line is: What's the end result?

- **Say:** The key to straightforward communication is not to play games, but to be up-front with people. This action is people smart because the other person doesn't have to be a mind reader.

- **Ask** participants why they think it can be difficult to speak our minds so that we are clear to someone else.

- **Show Slide #20:** Barriers to Speaking Your Mind.

- **Emphasize** the points participants did and did not make.

WORKBOOK p. 21

Expressing Yourself Clearly   **21**

When You Want to Be Direct

In situations where you want to speak up in a straightforward way, here are three tips to keep in mind:

Say "I," not "you."

I statements convey that you "own" your message.

Try *"I think that . . ."* rather than *"Don't you think . . ."* and *"My opinion is . . ."* rather than *"You are. . . ."*

Describe, don't blame.

Say what you think or feel in a clear, direct way instead of speaking judgmentally or sarcastically.

Try *"I disagree"* rather than *"You've got it wrong"* and *"I'm uncomfortable with the direction we're taking"* rather than *"This approach is off the wall!"*

Tell, don't hint.

Give your perspective as a statement rather than asking leading or hinting questions.

Try *"It seems to me . . ."* rather than *"Why not. . . ?"* and *"My sense is . . ."* rather than *"Haven't you noticed. . . ?"*

- **Refer to Workbook, p. 21:** When You Want to Be Direct.

- **Tell** participants that, while there are times when it's fine to be indirect and subtle, it's important to be able to be straightforward when we need to be.

- **Review** the three tips and examples of direct and indirect statements.

- **Say:** In focusing on straightforward communication, we are looking at ways to speak up about our thoughts and feelings. When we turn to assertiveness, in the next module, we will look at ways to speak up about our wants and needs.

WORKBOOK p. 22

TRY IT: Experiments in Change

★★★

Select one of the following experiments. . . .

Owning Communication:

☐

Choose a specific work situation in which to practice making "I" statements (for example, a staff meeting). For a week, keep track of how often you speak in your own voice. Are you doing it more or less often than you want to? What makes it difficult for you to make "I" statements?

Checking for Understanding:

☐

Practice confirming understanding for a week. Whenever you've talked at length or have introduced a complicated subject, make a point of checking out the listener's understanding by asking questions such as, *"Was that clear?"* or *"So what do you think?"* Based on people's responses, would you say you're usually coming across clearly? If not, what changes could you try?

Orienting:

☐

Choose a specific assignment you want to give someone. Write, word for word, how you would explain the task to that person, incorporating the key elements of effective orientation (name and brief description of the task, example of the task, benefit of doing the task, and expected duration of the task). You may then want to try out your verbatim orientation on the person you chose, asking him or her how clear you were.

Being Straightforward:

☐

Keep a record of situations at work in which you were not up-front with someone else—when you hinted and hedged, but didn't say what was on your mind, or you brought up a different subject than the one you really wanted to raise. Think about the reasons why you were evasive. Select one or two situations that might arise again and plan how you can be more straightforward. Then try out your plan and see how it goes.

Closing

Time: 5 minutes; *References:* Workbook, p. 22.

- **Refer to Workbook, p. 22:** TRY IT: Experiments in Change.

- **Invite** them to select an "experiment in change" they plan to try in order to work on communicating clearly. [*If there is adequate time between sessions, have them work on a chosen experiment before the group reconvenes.*]

- **Summarize:** We have been looking at the PeopleSmart skill of communicating clearly. Being able to do this skill helps us to use the next skill, which is asserting needs.

Asserting Your Needs

Suggested Time: 60 minutes.

SLIDE #21: Asserting Your Needs

SLIDE #22: "Since people cannot read minds, you must tell them what you want."

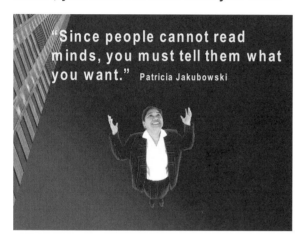

WORKBOOK p. 23

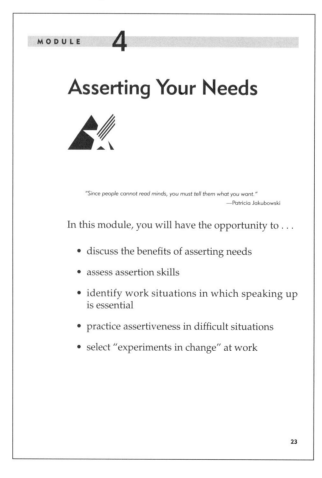

Introduction

Time: 5 minutes; *Materials:* PQ Scale; *References:* Slide #21, Asserting Your Needs, Slide #22, "Since people cannot read minds . . ."; Workbook, p. 23.

- **Show Slide #21:** Asserting Your Needs.

- **Refer to Workbook, p. 23:** Asserting Your Needs.

- **Review** the objectives.

- **Instruct** participants to rotate to a new partner, whom they will work with in this module.

- **Show Slide #22:** "Since people cannot read minds, you must tell them what you want."

- **Say:** In the last module, we focused on communicating clearly what we **think** and **feel.** In this module, we will focus on how to tell others what we **want**—and **do not want.**

- **Refer participants to PQ Scale:** PeopleSmart Skill 3.

- **Ask** participants to review their strengths and weaknesses for PeopleSmart Skill 3.

- **Ask:** How many of you rated yourselves as having some weaknesses at being assertive?

Video Clip 1: Asserting Your Needs

Video: Asserting Your Needs

Time: 10 minutes; *References:* Video clip #1.

- **Say:** Let's look at an example of someone trying to assert his needs. In the video you're about to see, Allysa, a project manager, wants Timothy, a team member, to work over the weekend. Timothy refuses. Tell me what you think about the way they both handle the situation.

- **Show Video Clip #1:** Asserting Your Needs.

- **Obtain reactions** to Timothy's assertiveness. Accept all reactions, positive and negative.

- **Debrief** by pointing out that Timothy was very clear and direct about his needs in this situation. Acknowledge that his behavior may have been "risky."

- **Optional:** Obtain reactions to Allysa's efforts to be assertive with Timothy. Generally, participants will see Timothy as much more effective in being direct and standing his ground.

- **Say:** Now that we've watched Timothy's and Alyssa's situation, let's turn to some of your own situations.

WORKBOOK p. 24

---

24   *PeopleSmart: Participant Workbook*

Practicing Assertiveness

★★★

One situation in which I'd like to be more assertive about saying "no" or expecting someone else to do something I need is . . .

❑ asking my boss for help in prioritizing my workload

❑ dealing with excessive overtime and work travel

❑ refusing coworkers' requests for help with tasks that are not in my job description

❑ receiving slow service from a supplier

❑ letting a client know that his or her "humor" is offensive to me

❑ turning down a subordinate's request

❑ other: _____

What exactly do I want in this situation? How insistent am I? What reasons would I give for my refusal or request?

_____

_____

_____

_____

_____

_____

_____

_____

_____

_____

_____

_____

_____

_____

_____

SLIDE #23: You Need to Decide ...

You Need to Decide

Time: 15 minutes; *References:* Slide #23, You Need to Decide; Workbook, p. 24.

- **Refer to Workbook, p. 24:** Practicing Assertiveness.

- **Instruct** them to choose a work situation in which they would like to be more assertive about their needs, using the checklist of situations as a guide. Tell them not to do the second part of the exercise at the bottom of the page yet.

- **Show Slide #23:** You Need to Decide. . . .

- **Say:** Assertiveness begins with ourselves. We need to be *clear* about exactly what we want. Vague wishes about how others should behave do not bring results. So you need to think through *what you want,* not just what you don't like about someone's behavior. For example, instead of being unhappy that someone is always interrupting you, you may want the person to let you finish your sentences before he or she responds. In order to clarify that, you first need to think through what you want.

- **Say:** You also need to decide *how insistent you are.* If you think of your possible level of insistence as being on a 1 to 10 scale, how strongly do you feel about your present need? Your decision will determine the language you will use to express your need. If you feel that your need is a 10, you will not want to sound like a 1 (and vice versa). There will also be times when you need to identify a brief reason for your refusal of a request. Sharing a rationale is not the same as offering excuses. Keep your reasons clear and simple.

- **Ask** participants: How many of you are not completely clear about these three decisions for the situation you chose?

- **Invite** one or two participants who are unclear about their decisions to describe the situations they chose. Choose one situation, making sure it actually calls for asserting one's needs (versus, for example, giving feedback to someone). Interview the participant to help him or her get as clear as possible what he or she wants from the other person. Ask questions like: "If this person were doing just what you want, what would we see?" If the person has difficulty being clear, point out that it is not unusual for us to find it easier to say what we don't want than what we do. However, if we can't get clear with ourselves what we want, we will not be able to be clear to someone else. If no one acknowledges being unclear, you may give a brief example of how the three decisions apply to a situation, such as feeling that meetings in your department run too long (e.g., one person might want a time limit on the meetings, while another might want participants to give input ahead of time on key agenda items).

- **Instruct** participants to write down their own decisions in the space at the bottom of Workbook page 24.

- **Say:** It's not only being clear about what we want that's important, but how we communicate it to another person.

SLIDE #24: Communicating Assertively

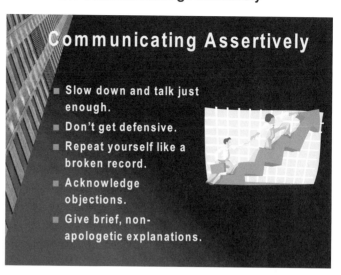

WORKBOOK p. 25

Asserting Your Needs   **25**

Communicating Assertively

- Take a deep breath, slow yourself down, and talk just enough to express your wishes.

- Communicate your position, using phrases such as:

  "I would appreciate it if you . . ."

  "I will not . . ."

  "It would be great if you . . ."

  "I will have to . . ."

  "Please . . ."

  "I would prefer that you . . ."

  "It works best for me if . . ."

  "I've decided not to . . ."

- Give brief, non-apologetic explanations for your position. Stop talking after giving your reason.

  "I can't discuss it right now because I have a deadline to meet."

- Don't get defensive, caught up in power struggles, or blow your cool.

- Repeat yourself like a "broken record."

  Calmly restate what you've said.

  Say the same thing in new words.

- When you hear objections, use phrases like:

  "That may be."

  "We see it differently."

  "That's true, and. . . ."

  "I realize how important this is to you, and. . . ."

Communicating Assertively

Time: 15 minutes; *Materials:* Director's clapboard (optional); *References:* Slide #24, Communicating Assertively; Workbook, p. 25.

- **Show Slide #24:** Communicating Assertively.

- **Explain** that you can remain calm and confident by slowing yourself down, speaking briefly and non-defensively, and staying focused on what you want to achieve, rather than responding to everything else that's being said. When people don't keep their word, you can remind them what has been agreed, or ask again for a commitment.

- **Refer to Workbook, p. 25:** Communicating Assertively.

- **Ask** participants to study the tips, then ask for their questions or reactions to them.

- **Say:** Let's see how these tips might look in action.

- **Invite** one of the participants who has already shared a description of his or her situation to assist you in a demonstration. Let the person know that *you* will be the one in the "hot seat" in this demonstration.

- **Ask** the designated participant to portray the other person in a role play of his or her situation. Offer to take the role of the participant. Obtain as much information as you need in order to portray the person realistically. Before beginning the role play, ask the group for advice on how to start off on the right foot. Listen to a few proposals. Act out those ideas about starting off the conversation that are consistent with good assertiveness skills. Then stop. Use the clapboard as a film director would to start and stop the role-play action.

- **Ask** the other person to give you a hard time. Again ask for advice from the group. Employ suggestions that help you to remain calm, confident, and persistent.

- **Debrief** by asking participants how you used the assertive communication behaviors.

- **Say:** Now you will have a chance to practice assertiveness in your own situations.

WORKBOOK p. 24

Practicing Assertiveness

⋆✦★

One situation in which I'd like to be more assertive about saying "no" or expecting someone else to do something I need is . . .

❑ asking my boss for help in prioritizing my workload

❑ dealing with excessive overtime and work travel

❑ refusing coworkers' requests for help with tasks that are not in my job description

❑ receiving slow service from a supplier

❑ letting a client know that his or her "humor" is offensive to me

❑ turning down a subordinate's request

❑ other: _____

What exactly do I want in this situation? How insistent am I? What reasons would I give for my refusal or request?

_____

_____

_____

_____

_____

_____

_____

_____

_____

_____

_____

_____

_____

WORKBOOK p. 25

Communicating Assertively

⋆✦★

- Take a deep breath, slow yourself down, and talk just enough to express your wishes.

- Communicate your position, using phrases such as:

    "I would appreciate it if you . . ."

    "I will not . . ."

    "It would be great if you . . ."

    "I will have to . . ."

    "Please . . ."

    "I would prefer that you . . ."

    "It works best for me if . . ."

    "I've decided not to . . ."

- Give brief, non-apologetic explanations for your position. Stop talking after giving your reason.

    "I can't discuss it right now because I have a deadline to meet."

- Don't get defensive, caught up in power struggles, or blow your cool.

- Repeat yourself like a "broken record."

    Calmly restate what you've said.

    Say the same thing in new words.

- When you hear objections, use phrases like:

    "That may be."

    "We see it differently."

    "That's true, and. . . ."

    "I realize how important this is to you, and. . . ."

Practicing Assertiveness

Time: 10 minutes: *References:* Workbook, pp. 24–25.

- **Instruct** participants to pair with their partners.

- **Instruct** each pair to discuss their selected situations and what they want (from page 24 in the Workbook). Then have them enlist their partner to be the other person so that they can rehearse how they might deal more assertively with the situation. Before beginning the rehearsal, suggest the participants refer to Workbook page 25: Communicating Assertively, and use the coaching tips as a "crib sheet." [*If time is limited, have each pair do only one role play.*]

- **Instruct** them to debrief with each other, using the tips as a basis for feedback.

WORKBOOK p. 26

TRY IT: Experiments in Change

⋆★★

Select one of the following experiments. . . .

Refusing Unwanted Requests:

☐

Make a list of requests people make of you that are a burden. Review the list and select one or two requests that you will refuse in the next week. Think about how you will politely, but firmly, inform someone of your need to say "no," then carry out your plan. What happened? Did you feel less guilty than you thought you would?

Making Clear Requests:

☐

Review the requests you want to make of others to help you meet your own needs at work. Select one or two. Get clear in your mind what you specifically want. Formulate each request so that it is as reasonable as possible for the person you will ask, then make your request(s). Did you receive a positive response? Are you happy with the support you obtained?

Responding to Objections:

☐

Take one of the following strategies and practice it for one week with a variety of people in various work situations. Work on it until it becomes second-nature:

- Repeat yourself rather than respond to someone's remarks.
- Avoid arguments with others by using phrases such as *"That may be," "We see it differently,"* and *"That's true, and. . . ."*
- Give brief, non-apologetic explanations for your position.

Persisting:

☐

Work on your persistence. Identify times you give up too easily or flip-flop on an issue on a day-to-day basis. Make a small list of decisions you would like to stick to in the coming week. After the week is up, look over your list and give yourself a grade: A = stuck to my guns; B = persisted most of the time; C = persisted some of the time; D = gave up.

Closing

Time: 5 minutes: *References:* Workbook, p. 26.

- **Refer to Workbook, p. 26:** TRY IT: Experiments in Change.

- **Encourage** them to select an "experiment in change" for asserting their needs. (If there is adequate time between sessions, have them work on a chosen experiment before the group reconvenes.)

- **Say:** Assertiveness gets easier with practice, so I hope you will test the waters by trying out these skills. Our next module deals with exchanging feedback.

Exchanging Feedback

Suggested Time: 60 minutes.

PQ
Scale

SLIDE #25: Exchanging Feedback

Exchanging Feedback

SLIDE #26: "Flatter me . . ."

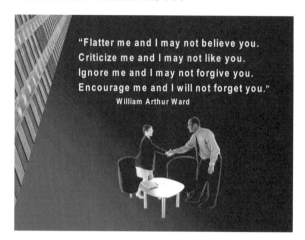

"Flatter me and I may not believe you.
Criticize me and I may not like you.
Ignore me and I may not forgive you.
Encourage me and I will not forget you."
William Arthur Ward

WORKBOOK p. 27

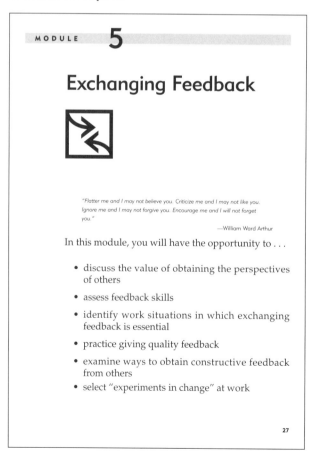

MODULE **5**

Exchanging Feedback

*"Flatter me and I may not believe you. Criticize me and I may not like you.
Ignore me and I may not forgive you. Encourage me and I will not forget
you."*

—William Ward Arthur

In this module, you will have the opportunity to . . .

- discuss the value of obtaining the perspectives
  of others

- assess feedback skills

- identify work situations in which exchanging
  feedback is essential

- practice giving quality feedback

- examine ways to obtain constructive feedback
  from others

- select "experiments in change" at work

27

Introduction

Time: 5 minutes; *Materials:* PQ Scale; *References:* Slide #25, Exchanging Feedback, Slide #26, "Flatter me . . ."; Workbook, p. 27.

- **Show Slide #25:** Exchanging Feedback.
- **Say:** Giving and requesting feedback effectively is the next people smart skill.
- **Show Slide #26:** "Flatter me. . . ."
- **Point out** that good feedback is not flattery or blatant criticism. *No* feedback is ignoring. Effective feedback is encouraging.
- **Instruct** participants to rotate to a new partner.
- **Say:** Let's look at the objectives for this module.
- **Refer to Workbook, p. 27:** Exchanging Feedback.
- **Review** objectives.
- **Refer participants to PQ Scale:** PeopleSmart Skill 4.
- **Invite** participants to review their strengths and weaknesses for PeopleSmart Skill 4.

Candy prize

Flip Chart: How Many Squares?

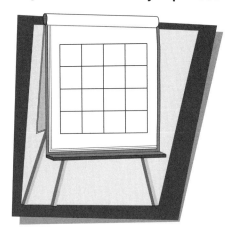

WORKBOOK p. 28

How Many Squares?*

★★★

My answer is: _____

_____

*Based on "Count the Squares," in *The Big Book of Business Games* by John Newstrom and Edward Scannell.

The Perspectives of Others

Time: 15 minutes; *Materials:* Candy; Prepared flip chart, "How Many Squares";
References: Slide #27, The Perspectives of Others; Workbook, p. 28; Video Clip #2,
A Feedback Request.

- **Show flip chart:** How Many Squares?

- **Ask:** How many squares do you see?

- **Refer to Workbook, p. 28:** How Many Squares?

- **Instruct** participants that they have twenty seconds to come up with their answers, which they should silently write down. Then ask people to call out their answers. Most participants will say 16 or 17. A few will go higher. If the correct answer (30) is given, give a token prize to the winner. To win, the participant must show, on the flip chart, how he or she computed the answer. If no one comes up with the correct answer, inform participants that the figure contains thirty squares. The outline of the entire box contains one square. And there are twenty-nine squares within the large box.

- **Explain and show** on the flip chart that there are, of course, sixteen small squares within the large box. There are also nine squares consisting of boxes of four 2 × 2 squares. They include the four quadrants of the large box and five more boxes of four (the quadrant in the middle of the large box and the four that are at the box edge and inset from the corners). There are also four boxes of nine 3 × 3 squares. Add these (5 + 4 + 4 = 13) to the original seventeen and you have thirty. (You may use different color marking pens to identify the nine 2 × 2 squares and the four 3 × 3 squares.)

- **Point out:** There are squares that many of you were unable to see without using the perspectives of others. This is true not only about squares in a drawing, but also about ways of seeing and understanding ourselves.

SLIDE #27: The Perspectives of Others

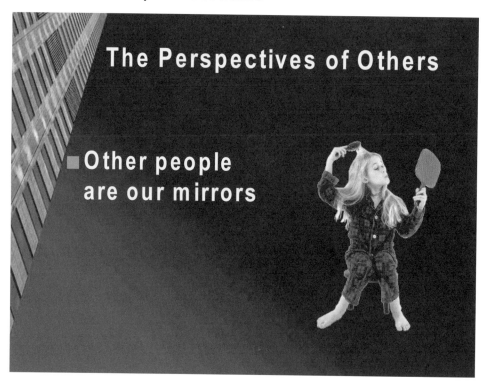

Video Clip #2: A Feedback Request

- **Show Slide #27:** The Perspectives of Others.

- **Say:** We don't always see what others see. We all have blind spots. For example, what *can't* the young woman in the slide see? (Participants will recognize that she cannot see her back.) It pays to get the perspective of others. Other people are our mirrors. It's helpful to know of people's reactions, even if those reactions are biased, inaccurate, or simply not helpful. At least you know what you're up against. But in the real world, it's not always easy to get others' perspectives.

- **Say:** Let's look at a real-world example of how it can be difficult to get honest feedback.

- **Say:** In the following video clip, Allan, the boss, seeks feedback from Paige on his presentation. See what you think of the feedback he receives from her.

- **Show Video Clip #2:** A Feedback Request.

- **Ask:** What do you think of the quality of the feedback Allan received from Paige? (Participants will readily respond that it was not helpful, misleading, etc.).

- **Ask:** Why do you think Paige's feedback was so poor? Briefly discuss responses.

- **Say:** This was a missed opportunity to receive feedback. This happens in the real world all the time. We don't always encourage others to tell us openly and honestly about areas of feedback that might be useful to us. But you will have that opportunity right now.

SLIDE #28: You Remind Me of . . .

WORKBOOK p. 29

Exchanging Feedback   **29**

Partner Feedback

★★★

Directions

From the list below, select the animal that most resembles your partner, considering both physical characteristics and personal qualities. Do *not* show your selection to your partner.

- ❏ Lion
- ❏ Squirrel
- ❏ Monkey
- ❏ Tiger
- ❏ Giraffe
- ❏ Kangaroo
- ❏ Bear (type?)
- ❏ Cat (type?)
- ❏ Dog (type?)
- ❏ Bird (type?)
- ❏ Other: _____

Partner Feedback

Time: 15 minutes; *References:* Slide #28, "You Remind Me of . . .", Slide #29, Reasons People Withhold Feedback, Slide #30, Six Ways to Encourage Feedback; Workbook, pp. 29, 30.

- **Show Slide #28:** You Remind Me of. . . .
- **Refer to Workbook, p. 29:** Partner Feedback.
- **Instruct** them to review the list and select an animal that can best be compared to their partner. (They may also choose an animal not on the list.) Suggest they consider both physical characteristics and the individual's personality, to the extent that they are familiar with it. Tell them *not* to divulge their selection to their partner and to put the page out of sight. (Expect groans and resistance, including possible objections on the grounds that participants don't know each other well enough to give such feedback. Don't be pulled into a debate.)
- **Say:** Before you tell your partner the animal you have chosen, I have two questions for you.
- **Poll** the group, asking (1) How many of you are *eager* to tell your partner what animal you selected? Allow hands to be raised. Then ask: (2) How many are *eager* to hear what animal your partner selected? (Expect that more people will want to hear than tell.)
- **Say:** This is what we are up against every day. We *are* curious what people think about us, but other people may often withhold feedback from us . . . even though they always have some feedback that can be shared. When that feedback is withheld, we wind up guessing how others think of us. Some of us think the feedback is more positive than it really is. Some of us think the opposite. The best thing we can do to get an accurate picture is to **ask** for feedback more often. If we are proactive and ask for feedback, we are in a better position to know how others view us, rather than making guesses.

SLIDE #29: Reasons People Withhold Feedback

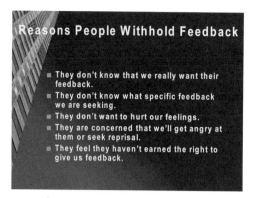

WORKBOOK p. 30

Reasons Why People Withhold Feedback from Us

★★★

- They don't know that we really want their feedback.

- They don't know what specific feedback we are seeking.

- They don't want to hurt our feelings.

- They are concerned that we will be angry at them or seek reprisal.

- They feel they haven't earned the right to give us feedback.

SLIDE #30: Six Ways to Encourage Feedback

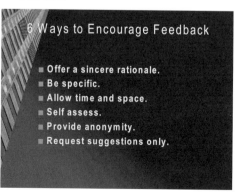

- **Ask.** Why are people often reluctant to share their feedback with us?
- **Discuss** participants' responses.
- **Show Slide #29:** Reasons People Withhold Feedback.
- **Refer to Workbook, p. 30:** Reasons Why People Withhold Feedback from Us.
- **Discuss** the fit with participants' responses.
- **Show Slide #30:** Six Ways to Encourage Feedback.
- **Discuss** the ways. (You may also give a brief illustration of how Allan, in the video clip, might have used each way to encourage more constructive feedback from Paige.)
- **Say:** You may now share your animal choices with your partners. But do so only if your partner successfully uses one or more of the strategies we've discussed to convince you that he or she really wants your feedback and won't hold it against you.
- **Invite** one or two participants to share how their partners encouraged them to reveal their animal choices.
- **Optional:** If participants are willing, invite them to share their animal choices with the group.
- **Point out** that, even when participants have just met each other in the course, they invariably come up with animal choices that are on target. This illustrates how much potentially valuable feedback is out there, waiting to be harvested.

WORKBOOK p. 31

Requesting Feedback

✦✦✦

Complete the action plan below for requesting feedback from someone on the job:

The person whose feedback I'd like is: _____.
I would like that person's feedback on: _____.
The strategies I'll use to invite feedback from that person are (write down specific phrases you can use after the strategy):

❑ Give a sincere rationale for my request. _____
_____
_____

❑ Be specific about the feedback I'm seeking. _____
_____
_____

❑ Give the person time to formulate his or her feedback.
_____
_____

❑ Self-assess to start the process. _____
_____
_____

❑ Find a way to make the feedback anonymous. _____
_____
_____

❑ Ask for suggestions only. _____
_____
_____

Requesting Feedback

Time: 5 minutes; *References:* Workbook, p. 31.

- **Refer to Workbook, p. 31:** Requesting Feedback.

- **Instruct** participants to identify someone in their work situation from whom they would like feedback and the kind of feedback they are seeking. Then ask them to use strategies from the list on the page to craft some phrases that they could use to invite the feedback. Encourage them to share their intentions with their partners.

- **Say:** So far we've been focusing on ways to request feedback. It's also important to be able to give feedback in a PeopleSmart way.

SLIDE #31: Giving Feedback

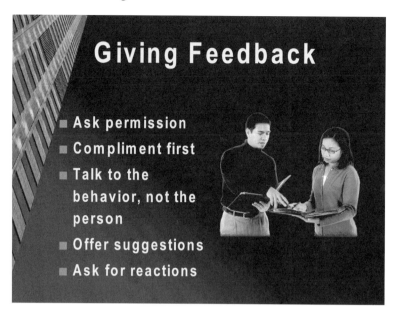

WORKBOOK p. 32

Giving Feedback

★✦★

Directions

1. Discuss the checklist below with your partner:

   • Ask permission.

   "Can we talk about what happened between us at the meeting?"

   "I have some things I'd like to say to you. Is this a good time?"

   • Compliment first.

   "I appreciate your. . . ."

   "I like the way you. . . ."

   • Talk to the behavior or action, not the person. Be specific.

   "I'm concerned about the way you handled your sales call. You focused on the features of the product but not on the benefits."

   • Offer suggestions.

   "I'd like to suggest that you. . . ."

   "I think I/you/we would be more effective if you. . . ."

   • Ask for reactions.

   "Is this helpful?"

   "How do you see it?"

2. Choose someone from your work environment to whom you'd like to give feedback: _____

3. Pretend your partner is that person and practice giving him or her constructive feedback.

4. Using the points on the checklist below as a guide, tell your partner how effective his or her feedback was.

Feedback Checklist

❑ Asked permission?

❑ Complimented first?

❑ Talked to the behavior or action, not the person?

❑ Was specific?

❑ Offered suggestions?

❑ Asked for reactions?

Giving Feedback

Time: 15 minutes; *References:* Slide #31, Giving Feedback; Workbook, p. 32.

- **Show Slide #31:** Giving Feedback.
- **Refer to Workbook, pp. 32:** Giving Feedback.
- **Instruct** participants to discuss the tips with their partners.
- **Point out** that some feedback situations tend to be formal, while some are informal.
- **Say:** While all these tips may not apply to every situation, which tips are you most "guilty," in your opinion, of not doing? Discuss responses.
- **Say:** Giving feedback is different from asserting your needs. When you offer feedback, don't insist that the other person change. Only give the feedback because you want to share your perceptions and be helpful.
- **Instruct** participants to choose someone from one of their four primary groups to whom they'd like to give feedback.
- **Demonstrate** giving feedback with a volunteer. Ask the volunteer to describe his or her situation. Role play the volunteer in his or her situation and show how he or she can give feedback effectively.
- **Ask** participants to identify how you used the tips on Workbook page 32.
- **Instruct** participants to pretend their partner is the person they chose and practice giving their feedback. Partners should then use the checklist on Workbook page 32 to describe how effective the feedback was. Each partner should take a turn practicing giving feedback. [*If time is short, do a single round.*]
- **Debrief** by inviting one or two participants to share which strategies they used.

WORKBOOK p. 33

TRY IT: Experiments in Change

⭑✦★

Select one of the following experiments. . . .

Requesting Feedback:

Identify someone from whom you'd like to get feedback. Approach the person and say, *"I'd like to improve my [select a quality, skill, or behavior]. Could you tell me how well I'm doing right now, and also let me know in the future if there's any change for the better or worse? Could we set a time to do this?"* Evaluate the results.

Giving Feedback:

Identify two people to whom you'd like to give feedback, even if you're not sure they want it. Select one of them to whom you have never given feedback or haven't done so in a long time. Think carefully about what you will say to that person; then find an opportunity to do so. What were the results?

Giving Feedback to a Difficult Person:

Think of someone you know who seems to have difficulty accepting feedback. Write down, word for word, three ways that you might ask that person for permission to share some feedback with him or her. Then write down two positive things about the person that you could share initially to improve your chances of being heard more easily in the future.

Improving Negative Feedback:

Think of someone to whom you have recently given negative feedback. If you did not give the person suggestions for improvement, write down two things that the person could do to improve. When you next have an opportunity to speak with the person, tell him or her, *"I've been thinking about the feedback I gave you the other day, and I'm not sure I was as helpful as I could have been. Could I take a moment to explain more clearly what I meant, and try to give you some concrete suggestions?"* If the person agrees, give your improved feedback, then check out whether this was helpful to the person.

Closing

Time: 5 minutes; *References:* Workbook, p. 33.

- **Refer to Workbook, p. 33:** TRY IT: Experiments in Change.
- **Invite** them to look at the experiments in change and consider trying one on the job. If there is adequate time between sessions, have them work on a chosen experiment before the group reconvenes.
- **Say:** The next PeopleSmart skill, influencing others, is one that many people find difficult.

Influencing Others

Suggested Time: 60 minutes.

SLIDE #32: Influencing Others

WORKBOOK p. 35

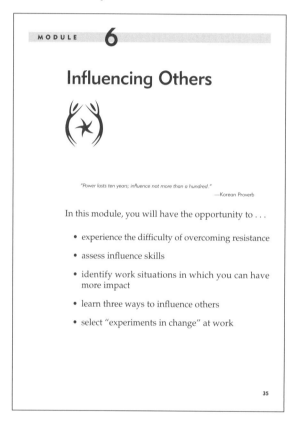

SLIDE #33: "Power lasts ten years . . ."

Introduction

Time: 5 minutes; *Materials:* PQ Scale; *References:* Slide #32, Influencing Others, Slide #33, "Power lasts ten years . . . "; Workbook, p. 35.

- **Show Slide #32:** Influencing Others.

- **Refer to Workbook, p. 35:** Influencing Others.

- **Review** objectives.

- **Show Slide #33:** "Power lasts ten years; influence not more than a hundred."

- **Ask** participants to interpret this proverb.

- **Explain:** Power involves controlling what others do. Its effect depends on how long the person in power lasts. Influence implies that the other person is choosing the action himself or herself. Influence thus lives beyond the life of the influencer.

- **Refer participants to PQ Scale:** PeopleSmart Skill 5.

- **Invite** them to take another look at their strengths and deficits for Skill 5.

Candy Prize

SLIDE #34: Reflection Questions

Reflection Questions

- Did you ask questions to better understand the person's point of view?

- Did you point out the benefits the person would receive if s/he followed your advice?

- Did you give the person time and space to mull over your proposal?

A Flawed Persuasion Effort

Time: 10 minutes; *Materials:* Candy prize; *References:* Slide #34, Reflection Questions.

- **Recruit** a volunteer and enlist him or her to be on the receiving end of your efforts to be persuasive. (**Note:** Recruit the volunteer ahead of time and agree on a scenario you will use for the exercise. Try to choose a situation that is relevant to participants' work roles or organizational mission.)

- **Explain** to participants that you are going to attempt to persuade the person (who should be very resistant) to adopt your point of view or proposal. Tell them that you will be operating under a specific constraint in your efforts and ask them to see if they can figure out what it is. (The constraint is that you will not be allowed to ask the person any questions.)

- **Begin.** Stop the role play when appropriate and offer a candy prize to the volunteer. Ask participants to give their feedback on your persuasion efforts. See whether anyone can identify what your particular constraint was.

- **Ask:** What else could I have done under these difficult circumstances?

- **Say:** We often try to convince people of something without finding out their needs, concerns, and objections. With this information, we are in a better position to point out how the other person will "benefit" from doing what we want him or her to do.

- **Briefly do a re-take** of the role play, showing how it would have started differently if you asked relevant questions. Obtain reactions to the difference.

- **Show Slide #34:** Reflection Questions.

- **Refer to** the three questions on the slide and discuss how they applied to your lack of success in the first round of the previous demonstration.

- **Say:** Now you'll have a chance to apply these questions to a situation of your own.

WORKBOOK p. 36

Analyzing a Personal Case Problem

★✦★

Directions

1. Think of someone you recently tried to persuade . . . without success. It may be
   a situation in which you wanted the person to adopt your advice, to change his
   or her mind, or to act in a certain way. *What were the details?*

   _____

   _____

   _____

   _____

   _____

   _____

2. Tell your partner about this experience. Then invite your partner to interview
   you, using these questions:

   • Did you ask questions to better understand the person's point of view?

   • Did you point out the benefits the other person would receive if he or she
     adopted your advice or changed his or her mind?

   • Did you give the person some time and space to mull over what you were
     proposing?

Analyzing a Personal Case Problem

Time: 10 minutes; *References:* Workbook, p. 36.

- **Refer to Workbook, p. 36:** Analyzing a Personal Case Problem.

- **Instruct** them to identify a recent situation in which they were unsuccessful at persuading another person. Ask them to record their situations in their workbooks and then to evaluate their efforts to influence the person with their partners, using the list of reflection questions.

- **Reconvene** the group to obtain reactions and questions. If you notice that participants focus more on the person who was resistant than on their own actions, point out that many people in this world are difficult, but the people smart thing to do is to look at what *you* might do to try to win them over, despite their resistance. Ask participants to share which of the three questions were most helpful to them.

SLIDE #35: 4 Ways to Be Open to Resistance

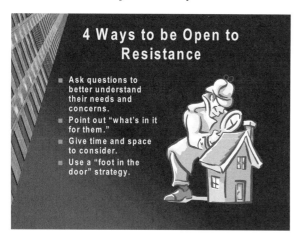

SLIDE #36: Getting a Foot in the Door

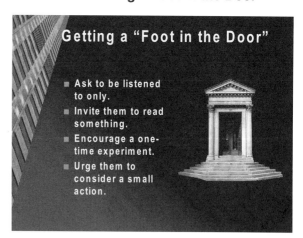

WORKBOOK p. 37

Influencing Others   **37**

An Example of Influence

A supervisor was urging the toll booth collectors to be friendlier to drivers when they paid a toll. The collectors resisted. "If we talk like they do in stores and hotels these days," they argued, "the public will think we're crazy or just forced to do it. It's not what people expect." The supervisor wisely responded: "Okay, I'll make a deal with you.

"Try to say hello or say thank you or smile at the customers for one week, and we'll get back together to see if it works for you."

The next week, the toll collectors reported that they did not know what effect the experiment had on the customers, but they all reported that they liked their jobs better.

(No doubt, the customers returned their friendliness in kind.)

PeopleSmart Persuasion

Time: 10 minutes; *References:* Slide #35, Four Ways to Be Open to Resistance, Slide #36, Getting a Foot in the Door; Workbook, p. 37.

- **Say:** In a sense, being able to influence others means being *open to resistance* rather than fighting or ignoring it. Let's look at three strategies that can help us do this.

- **Show Slide #35:** Four Ways to Be Open to Resistance.

- **Review** the four strategies.

- **Show Slide #36:** Getting a Foot in the Door.

- **Say:** When you encounter resistance, instead of pushing or giving up, it helps to encourage the person to take a small step in the direction you want him or her to go. We call this "getting a foot in the door" (as opposed to a door in the face!).

- **Discuss** the ways to get a foot in the door. Point out how you might have used them, either in your own unsuccessful influence effort, or in the opening demonstration in this module.

- **Refer to Workbook, p. 37:** An Example of Influence.

- **Recruit a** volunteer to read aloud the example.

- **Ask participants:** Which "foot in the door" strategy did the supervisor use? (Explain, if necessary, that he invited them to try an experiment or pilot.)

- **Say:** Now you will have a chance to practice these influence strategies.

WORKBOOK p. 38

Practicing Influence Skills

Directions

Identify a situation from the list below or create one yourself.

1. You have been trying to convince a person who reports to you to take more initiative. That may include actions such as:

   - suggesting a better way to do something

   - when possible, undertaking a small project without waiting to be assigned to do it

   - giving you feedback about your behavior as a manager

   So far, the person has been reluctant to do this. Try to change his or her mind.

2. You want your busy boss to give you performance feedback more frequently. S/He feels that you are doing a great job and don't need the extra feedback. Your boss is also overwhelmed with his/her own responsibilities. See whether you can get the boss to commit him- or herself to what you want.

3. Someone on your team disagrees with your insistence that no important decisions are made by individuals unless they are checked out with everyone else on the team. Persuade him/her to agree with you.

4. One of your customers continues to use a service or product from another provider that you know is inferior to your own. Convince him/her to give you the business.

Ask your partner to portray the person you want to influence. Use the opportunity to practice the influence skills that have been discussed so far in this module.

When you are finished, invite your partner to give you feedback about your influence skills.

Practicing Influence Skills

Time: 10 minutes; *References:* Workbook, p. 38.

- **Refer to Workbook, p. 38:** Practicing Influence Skills.

- **Instruct** participants to practice influencing by choosing one of the work situations listed, or another from their own experience, and role playing with their partners. Instruct the person being influenced to resist and the persuaders to use the tips and techniques they have learned.

- **Set up** the practice by dividing participants into four subgroups.

- **Assign** one scenario to each group. Instruct the groups to agree on roles for the practice, with those not playing the protagonists acting as coaches for the two who are taking those roles.

- **Debrief** by asking all the participants whether anyone was faced with a really good persuader. Invite one or two participants to share.

WORKBOOK p. 39

Identifying an Opportunity to Influence Others

★★★

Directions

1. Identify a situation coming up in which you want to influence someone. (It can be the same situation in which you previously failed, or a new one.) Describe it:

   _____

   _____

   _____

   _____

   _____

   _____

2. Consult with your partner and decide which of the following strategies you would use to influence this person. How could you use the strategy?

   • Ask questions to better understand the person's needs and concerns.

   • Point out benefits to the other person if he or she adopts your idea.

   • Give the person time and space to consider your proposal.

   • Use a "foot in the door" strategy:

     Ask the person to listen to your views without pressure to respond.

     Invite the person to read something.

     Encourage a one-time experiment.

     Urge the person to consider a small action.

Identifying an Influence Opportunity

Time: 10 minutes; *References:* Workbook, p. 39.

- **Refer to Workbook, p. 39:** Identifying an Opportunity to Influence Others.

- **Ask** each participant to identify a situation coming up in which he or she wants to be more influential with someone. [*If time is short, have only one partner choose a situation.*]

- **Invite** participants to consult with their partners about which influence strategies they would use.

- **Debrief** by asking whether anyone has a new "game plan" as a result of their consultation.

WORKBOOK p. 40

TRY IT: Experiments in Change

★★★

Select one of the following experiments. . . .

Developing Rapport:

☐

Make it a special project to take time to develop rapport with someone you want to influence. Think about how to show interest in that person. Also, think of how you can be more interesting to him or her. Avoid giving advice during this time. Develop trust by letting the person see that you are not out to remake him or her in your image. Also, accentuate the positive. Seize every opportunity to compliment the person. It's hard to influence someone you have criticized a lot.

Asking Questions:

☐

Think of two people you want to influence as your "customers." Devote a week to working on asking questions rather than giving advice. Learn more about their needs, preferences, and wishes, and store that information for later use.

Practicing Patience:

☐

For one week, try to lessen your eagerness to influence people right away. Every time you are in a situation in which you want to be persuasive, try to be patient with yourself and with others. Give yourself time to think before you speak, and give others the space and elbow room to consider what you're saying without responding right away. See whether you like the results.

Being Persuasive:

☐

Identify a person to whom you want to be more persuasive. Develop a plan for encouraging that person to accept your idea. Prepare yourself with information about the benefits of your ideas. Think about how you might make your suggestions more appealing by using good examples, re-framing, and metaphors. Try out your plan.

Closing

Time: 5 minutes; *References:* Workbook, p. 40.

- **Refer to Workbook, p. 40:** TRY IT: Experiments in Change.

- **Instruct** them to look over the "experiments in change" and consider trying one back on the job. If there is adequate time between sessions, have them try a chosen experiment before the group reconvenes.

- **Summarize:** Influencing is a complex skill that builds on the earlier PeopleSmart skills of understanding people and communicating clearly. The next skill, resolving conflict, is another complex skill that many people find challenging.

Resolving Conflict

Suggested Time: 90 minutes.

Flip Chart: Images of Conflict

SLIDE #37: Resolving Conflict

SLIDE #38: "As long as you keep a person down . . ."

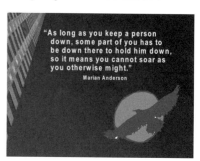

WORKBOOK p. 41

MODULE **7**

Resolving Conflict

"As long as you keep a person down, some part of you has to be down there to hold him down, so it means you cannot soar as you otherwise might."
—Marian Anderson

You will have the opportunity to . . .

- examine feelings about conflict and preferences for dealing with it

- assess conflict resolution skills

- identify work situations in which conflict resolution is essential

- examine ways to understand the interests of the other side and use them to create resolution

- practice win-win conflict resolution

- select "experiments in change" at work

41

Introduction

Time: 10 minutes: *Materials:* Prepared flip chart, Images of Conflict; PQ Scale; *References:* Slide #37, Resolving Conflict; Slide #38, "As long as you keep a person down. . . ."; Workbook, p. 41.

- **Show Slide #37:** Resolving Conflict.

- **Show Slide #38:** "As long as you keep a person down. . . ."

- **Say:** The next PeopleSmart skill, resolving conflict, without "keeping a person down," is a challenging one for all of us.

- **Refer to Workbook, p. 41:** Resolving Conflict.

- **Review** objectives.

- **Say:** For the next hour and a half, we will be focusing on conflict, something with which we all have some powerful associations.

- **Instruct** participants to free associate to the word "conflict" by sharing the images, words, or feelings that come to mind.

- **Chart** responses by recording them in two columns, positive and negative, but do not reveal how you are categorizing the responses. Expect that almost all associations will be negative.

- **Say:** We bring to most conflict situations a negative attitude.

- **Ask:** How can we view conflict positively?

- **Obtain responses,** using the points below as a guide:

  Conflicts can create an opportunity to resolve things that have been brewing under the surface.

  Conflicts can lead to new ideas.

  Conflicts can bring people closer together.

  (You may offer the analogy that conflict, at best, is like an oyster struggling with a grain of sand to produce a pearl.)

- **Refer participants to PQ Scale:** PeopleSmart Skill 6.

- **Ask** them to take another look at their strengths and deficits.

Flip Chart: Conflict Styles at Work

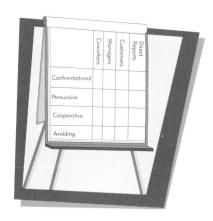

WORKBOOK p. 42

42   *PeopleSmart: Participant Workbook*

Comfort with Conflict

★ ★ ★

Directions

1. Circle the number below that describes how comfortable you are with conflict most of the time:

Uncomfortable . . . . Comfortable

| 1 | 2 | 3 | 4 | 5 |

2. Discuss with your partner what makes you comfortable and uncomfortable in conflict situations.

3. Thumb wrestle with your partner until one of you wins two out of three rounds.

4. Based on your thumb wrestling experience, answer the following questions:

- Who liked it?

- Who disliked it?

- Who was competitive?

- Who was sneaky?

- Who was defensive?

- Who was easygoing?

SLIDE #39: Four Styles of Conflict

Conflict Styles

Time: 15 minutes; *Materials:* Prepared flip chart, Conflict Styles at Work; *References:* Slide #39, Four Styles of Conflict; Workbook, pp. 42–44.

- **Instruct** participants to rotate to a new partner.
- **Refer to Workbook, p. 42:** Comfort with Conflict.
- **Say:** You and your new partner will now have an opportunity to delve into conflict with each other.
- **Provide** the following instructions:

  First, on your own, rate your comfort level with conflict.

  Then, compare ratings with your partner and discuss what makes you comfortable and uncomfortable in conflict situations. This module is about building comfort with conflict. That's important because people smart individuals are proactive in conflict situations.

  Next, thumb wrestle with your partner until one of you wins two out of three rounds. (Demonstrate thumb wrestling with a volunteer.)

  Finally, debrief the thumb wrestling experience with your partner, using the checklist questions.

- **Reconvene** the entire group to debrief the checklist questions. Explain that how we answer these questions is connected to our approach to conflict.
- **Show Slide #39:** Four Styles of Conflict.
- **Say:** The four styles reflect a continuum of the ways people approach conflict, with confrontational and avoiding styles at the extremes.

  Confrontational people tend to be aggressive, "in your face" types, who can be bullying or judgmental (provide an example, such as a well-known political, entertainment, or sports personality).

  Persuasive individuals are assertive and don't hesitate to stand up for themselves (provide an example).

  Cooperative types are comfortable doing more listening than talking. They are often willing to be conciliatory, but will speak up if an issue is important to them (provide an example).

  Avoiding people would prefer to cross the street rather than engage in a conflict. They may withdraw or accept situations they dislike, rather than speak up (provide an example).

- **Say:** Our styles may vary with the situation. For example, an employee may be very meek and avoiding with his aggressive boss, but become confrontational at home with his family. This pattern has been called "kicking the dog."

WORKBOOK p. 43

Four Styles of Conflict

★✦✱

CONFRONTATIONAL people tend to be aggressive, "in your face" types who can be bullying or judgmental.

PERSUASIVE individuals are assertive and don't hesitate to stand up for themselves.

COOPERATIVE types are comfortable doing more listening than talking. They are often willing to be conciliatory, but will speak up if an issue is important to them.

AVOIDING people would prefer to cross the street rather than engage in a conflict. They may withdraw or accept situations they dislike, rather than speak up.

In order to handle conflicts effectively, it's important to expand our range of styles and to recognize the styles we encounter in others that may pose difficulty for us.

My conflict style is usually:

_____ with my coworkers

_____ with my manager

_____ with my customers

_____ with my direct reports

WORKBOOK p. 44

Handling the Four Styles of Conflict

★✦✱

Confrontational

Don't give in to intimidation. Calmly ask the person to "lower the volume" (*"I think we'll do better if we slow down and hear each other out"*).

Persuasive

Acknowledge the person's points without abandoning your own interests (*"What you're saying makes good sense. Perhaps you haven't also considered that . . ."*).

Cooperative

Draw out additional concerns the person may have, in addition to sharing your own (*"Is there anything else that's important to you that we haven't touched on?"*).

Avoiding

Create a safe environment for sharing needs and concerns (*"As an experiment, could we spend the next five minutes imagining what each of us would walk away with in the best of all possible worlds?"*).

- **Refer to Workbook, p. 43:** Four Styles of Conflict.
- **Instruct** them to identify their conflict styles in each of their primary relationships.
- **Poll** the group, by show of hands, for representation of each conflict style (the one each person *primarily* uses) in each relationship.
- **Chart** a tally of the results and discuss the trends. (Often, for example, people are more likely to be cooperative or avoiding with managers and persuasive with coworkers.)
- **Say:** In order to handle conflicts effectively, it's important to expand our range of styles and to recognize the styles we encounter in others that pose difficulty for us.
- **Refer to Workbook, p. 44:** Handling the Four Styles of Conflict.
- **Invite participants** to look over the tips for handling the different styles.
- **Point out** that, when we encounter people at the extremes of the continuum (i.e., confrontational or avoiding), we may need to adjust our own styles "up or down" to meet their approach. So in dealing with a confrontational person, you might do best to take a persuasive approach and in dealing with an avoiding person, a cooperative one.
- **Say:** The next exercise will let you put your styles into action.

SLIDE #40: The Case of the Ugli Oranges

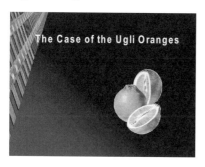

WORKBOOK p. 45

Resolving Conflict   **45**

Role for Dr. Roland in the Ugli Orange Case*

You are Dr. P. W. Roland. You work as a research biologist for a pharmaceutical firm. The firm is under contract with the government to do research on methods to combat enemy uses of biological warfare.

Recently several World War II experimental nerve gas bombs were moved from the United States to a small island just off the U.S. coast in the Pacific. During transportation, two of the bombs developed leaks. The leaks are presently controlled, but government scientists believe the gas will permeate the bomb chambers within two weeks. They know of no method to prevent the gas from reaching the atmosphere and spreading to other islands, and very likely the West Coast as well. If this occurs, thousands of people will incur serious brain damage or die.

You've developed a synthetic vapor, which will neutralize the nerve gas if it is injected into the bomb chambers before the gas leaks out. The vapor is made with a chemical taken from the rind of the Ugli orange, a very rare fruit. Unfortunately, only 3,000 of these oranges were produced this season.

You have learned that a Mr. R. H. Cardoza, a fruit exporter in South America, is in possession of 3,000 Ugli oranges. The chemicals from the rinds of this number of oranges would be sufficient to neutralize the gas if the serum is developed and injected efficiently. You have also been informed that the rinds of these oranges are in good condition.

You have also learned that Dr. J. W. Jones is also urgently seeking purchase of Ugli oranges and is aware of Mr. Cardoza's possession of the 3,000 oranges available. Dr. Jones works for a firm with which your firm is highly competitive. There is a great deal of industrial espionage in the pharmaceutical industry. Over the years, your firm and Dr. Jones' firm have frequently sued each other for violations of industrial espionage laws and infringement of patent rights. Litigation is still in progress.

The Federal government has asked your firm for assistance. You've been authorized by your firm to approach Mr. Cardoza to purchase the 3,000 Ugli oranges. You have been told he will sell them to the highest bidder and your firm has authorized you to bid as high as $2 million for the rind of the oranges. Before approaching Mr. Cardoza, you have decided to talk with Dr. Jones to influence him so that he will not prevent you from purchasing the oranges.

*Used with the permission of Robert J. Heuse.

WORKBOOK p. 46

Role for Dr. Jones in the Ugli Orange Case*

You are Dr. John W. Jones, a biological research scientist employed by a pharmaceutical firm. You have recently developed a synthetic chemical useful for curing and preventing Rudosen, a disease contracted by pregnant women. If not caught in the first four weeks of pregnancy, Rudosen causes serious brain, eye, and ear damage to the unborn child. Recently, there has been an outbreak of Rudosen in your state and several thousand women have contracted the disease.

You have found, with volunteer victims, that your recently developed synthetic serum cures Rudosen in its early stages. Unfortunately, the serum is made from the juice of the Ugli orange, a very rare fruit. Only a small quantity, 3,000 of these oranges, were produced last season. No additional Ugli oranges will be available until next season, too late to cure the present Rudosen victims.

You've demonstrated that your synthetic serum is in no way harmful to pregnant women and it has no side effects. The Food and Drug Administration has approved the production and distribution of the serum as a cure for Rudosen. The present outbreak was unexpected and your firm had not planned on having the compound serum available for six months. Your firm holds the patent on the synthetic serum and it is expected to be a highly profitable product when it becomes generally available to the public.

You have recently been informed that Mr. R. H. Cardoza, a South American fruit exporter, is in possession of 3,000 Ugli oranges in good condition. If you could obtain the juice of all 3,000, you would be able to cure the present victims and provide sufficient inoculation for the remaining pregnant women in the state.

You have also learned that Dr. P. W. Roland is also urgently seeking Ugli oranges and is also aware of Mr. Cardoza's possession of the 3,000 oranges available. Dr. Roland is employed by a competitor pharmaceutical firm and has been working on biological warfare research for the past several years. There is a great deal of industrial espionage in the pharmaceutical industry. Over the years, Dr. Roland's firm and your firm have repeatedly sued each other for violation of industrial espionage laws and patent infringement. Litigation is still in progress.

You've been authorized by your firm to approach Mr. Cardoza to purchase the 3,000 Ugli oranges. You have been told he will sell them to the highest bidder. Your firm has authorized you to bid as high as $2 million to obtain the juice of the 3,000 available oranges. Before approaching Mr. Cardoza, you have decided to talk with Dr. Roland to influence him so that he will not prevent you from purchasing the oranges.

*Used with the permission of Robert J. Heuse.

The Case of the Ugli Oranges

Time: 15 minutes; *Materials:* two oranges (optional); *References:* Slide #40, The Case of the Ugli Oranges; Workbook, pp. 45–46.

- **Show Slide #40:** The Case of the Ugli Oranges.

- **Pair** participants with their partners.

- **Assign** one person the role of Dr. Roland and the other the role of Dr. Jones. (**Note:** Since they have just thumb-wrestled with their partners, you might ask them to measure their thumbs against each other's and assign the roles based on who has the larger and smaller thumb.)

- **Instruct** "Dr. Roland" to turn to Workbook page 45: Role for Dr. Roland, and "Dr. Jones" to turn to Workbook page 46: Role for Dr. Jones.

- **Tell** them to read their prescribed roles (but not their partners'). Allow adequate time for participants to absorb the background information.

- **Hold up** the oranges (if available) and say: "I am the owner of the remaining Ugli oranges. Now that you've read about your roles, spend about ten minutes meeting with your partner and decide on a course of action. I am strictly interested in making a profit and will sell my oranges to the highest bidder. Since my country is alien to yours, there is no way either government will assist you in obtaining the oranges from me. Assume that there is only one Dr. Roland and Dr. Jones in this room, even though several of you will portray each character, and assume there are no other parties interested in the oranges. When you have negotiated a successful solution, pick a spokesperson who will tell me what you plan to do. If you want to buy the oranges, what price will you offer me? To whom and how will the oranges be delivered?"

- **Instruct** each pair to signal you when they are ready to respond. Tell them to do their best to achieve a win/win solution. Stop the exercise after ten minutes or when about half the pairs have signaled.

- **Poll** the groups to find out how many are ready to make you an offer. Briefly ask the "stuck" pairs to describe the status of their negotiations.

- **Invite** a pair who has achieved a win/win solution to explain their plan. If they've succeeded, reward them with a pair of oranges. (If more than one pair has succeeded, ask them to share the oranges.)

- **Say:** A win/win solution to this conflict was completely possible: Dr. Roland gets the rinds, Dr. Jones, the juice. The only way to succeed was by getting the parties' real needs on the table. Creating a climate of information sharing is essential to this process.

SLIDE #41: Types of Conflicts

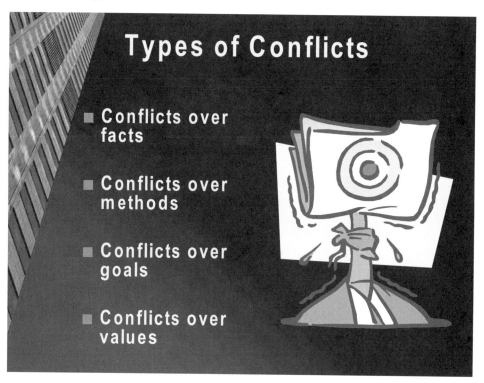

Video Clip #3: Resolving Conflict

Types of Conflicts

Time: 15 minutes; *References:* Slide: #41, Types of Conflicts; Video Clip #3, Resolving Conflict.

- **Show Slide #41:** Types of Conflicts.

- **Say:** One key step in conflict resolution is to recognize the type of conflict we're having.

- **Review** the four types of conflicts:

  Conflicts over facts are often really misunderstandings. The solution usually involves clarifying information. This was the case in the Ugli Orange exercise we just did. Once the facts are clear, a solution is easy to find.

  Conflicts over methods can often be solved by compromise, especially if both parties share the same ultimate goals, for example, a case where two managers want to improve productivity, but one wants to do so through incentives and the other through cracking down on abuse of sick leave. It may be possible to combine some of each approach.

  Conflicts over purposes or goals are often more difficult to solve. But goals that are different are not necessarily incompatible and it may be important to try to combine purposes when possible. For example, if one manager wants to improve productivity and the other morale, they may look for key areas where the two goals are compatible—such as uniting staff to out-produce a competing company.

  Conflicts over basic values are the hardest to solve (for example, abortion rights), and sometimes participants must agree to disagree.

- **Say:** Let's see whether you can identify which type of conflict is taking place in the next video clip.

- **Explain** that the clip features two characters they have seen before, Allan and Allysa, who are dealing with a conflict over desk space.

- **Show Video #3:** Resolving Conflict.

- **Ask:** What type of conflict was this?

- **Explain**, if necessary, that it was a conflict over methods. If participants insist it was a conflict over facts, you might point out that sharing a desk does involve some compromise, as you would not keep personal items, such as a change of clothing, in a shared desk. If they insist it was a conflict over goals, point out that it's unlikely that either protagonist really wanted to *prevent* anyone from having a desk.

- **Say:** Resolving this conflict looked almost too easy. But in real life, tempers can flare, even over something this simple. By asking questions, rather than launching into an argument, Allan gets the issues out in a way that makes it relatively easy to solve the conflict. And this is something that people often fail to do.

SLIDE #42: It's Always Worth Striving for Win/Win

SLIDE #43: Getting to Win/Win

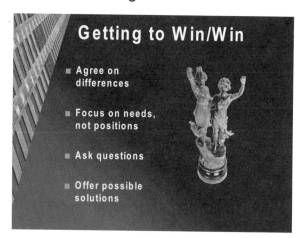

WORKBOOK p. 47

Resolving Conflict

47

Getting to Win/Win

★★★

1. Agree on your differences.

   "We seem to disagree about _____."

   "We've been fighting about _____ for quite a while."

   "As I understand it, you want _____ and I want _____. Would you agree?"

2. Focus on needs, not positions.

   "Let me explain what concerns me and you tell me what concerns you."

3. Ask questions.

   "What's important to you?"
   "What would you do if you were in my shoes?"
   "How did you come with that position?"
   "What else is important to you?"

4. Offer possible solutions.

   "Let's come up with some ideas together."
   "Would that idea work?"
   "What's our best idea?"
   "What exactly are we going to do? When?"

Getting to Win/Win

Time: 10 minutes; *References:* Slide #42, It's Always Worth Striving for Win/Win; Slide #43, Getting to Win/Win; Slide #44, Questions for Understanding Needs; Slide #45, Getting to Win/Win; Workbook, pp. 47–48.

- **Show Slide #42:** It's Always Worth Striving for Win/Win.

- **Say:** Not all work conflicts can result in win/win solutions, especially if they are about competing goals or values. But it's people smart to strive for them anyway.

- **Ask:** Do you agree? Why is this so? Obtain responses. Point out, if necessary, that a good relationship is preserved if the negotiation, although unsuccessful, was win/win oriented. Also, circumstances down the road may change. If a good relationship has been maintained, it allows the parties to seize upon the change and develop a win/win solution.

- **Show Slide #43:** Getting to Win/Win.

- **Say:** Feelings can run high in conflict situations, but it's important to stay positive and try to keep emotions in check. It may help to take time out and "go to the balcony" when necessary, in order to regain perspective and avoid being diverted from your goals. A good rule of thumb is to be *"soft on people and hard on problems."*

- **Explain** that these four steps allow you to be soft on people and hard on problems.

- **Say:** The first step is to *agree on differences.* That means identifying the conflict *we are having with each other,* rather than labeling or judging your counterpart. It may help to recognize the type of conflict going on. Doing so in a neutral and accurate way can be a powerful step toward lowering people's defenses in a conflict situation.

- **Refer to Workbook, p. 47:** Getting to Win/Win and ask them to look at Step 1.

- **Explain** that the quotes represent ways you can communicate to someone else that you are willing to work toward an agreement rather than just argue your own position.

- **Refer back to Slide #43:** Getting to Win/Win.

- **Say:** Let's look at the second step, "focus on needs, not positions."

- **Say:** In a typical conflict, each side takes a position, a stand about what they want. Often, people waste considerable time and effort trying to reconcile positions that are diametrically opposed. In reality, parties in a conflict also hold basic interests, which may be as important, or more important, to them than the positions they take. Interests are our needs, motivations, or reasons for our positions. When we can *understand and address the basic needs* each side brings to the table, we greatly expand the possibilities for reaching a win/win solution. (Give an example, e.g., a recent municipal transit strike was averted when the union

WORKBOOK p. 48

48   *PeopleSmart: Participant Workbook*

Questions for Understanding Needs

★ ★ ★

1. Review the list of sample conflict situations below. Either choose one that fits your experience or describe a conflict situation of your own:

   ❑ Conflict in an office with a coworker who has not behaved in a professional manner

   ❑ Conflict with a manager or coworker over a specific action plan or strategy for increasing business

   ❑ Conflict with direct reports on timeliness or organizational matters

   ❑ Conflict with a supplier over deliveries

   ❑ Conflict within a team over procedures

   ❑ Conflict with your manager over work/life balance issues

   ❑ Conflict with representatives from other companies over competitive practices

   ❑ Conflict within teams over inequities in work schedules

   ❑ Conflict with direct reports over quality of work

   ❑ Other: _____

   _____

2. Review the list of questions below and select the ones you would use to understand the other person's needs in your own situation:

   ❑ What do you want?

   ❑ Why do you want that?

   ❑ What's concerning you?

   ❑ What would you do if you were in my shoes?

   ❑ What makes that seem fair to you?

   ❑ What's the most important part of that for you?

   ❑ How would that benefit you?

   ❑ How did you come up with that position?

   ❑ What else matters to you in this situation?

SLIDE #44: Questions for Understanding Needs

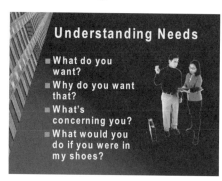

SLIDE #45: Getting to Win/Win

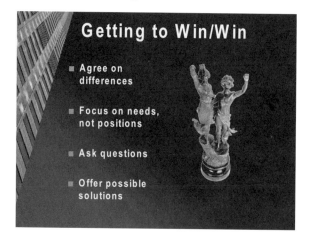

recognized that the city would lose face with constituents by giving raises, but could get away with a cost-of-living increase.)

- **Say:** The best way to uncover the other person's needs is Step 3, "Ask questions."

- **Show Slide #44:** Questions for Understanding Needs.

- **Discuss** the importance of asking good, open-ended questions in order to understand what others really have at stake in a conflict.

- **Refer to Workbook, p. 48:** Questions for Understanding Needs.

- **Instruct** participants to look at the items in section 2 as examples of good questions.

- **Show Slide #45:** Getting to Win/Win.

- **Say:** The fourth step to win/win is to generate solutions to the conflict.

- **Say:** Often, brainstorming is a good way to generate solutions. There are several different brainstorming methods, but they all involve listing potential solutions, without judging them off the bat, picking the most promising solutions, and making a plan to implement them. Brainstorming isn't hard. The hard part of conflict resolution is getting the real issues on the table.

Clapboard

SLIDE #46: The $20K Conflict

SLIDE #47: Questions for Understanding Needs

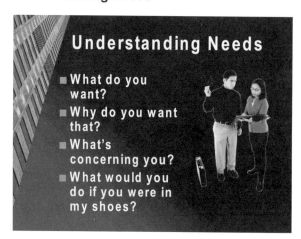

The $20K Conflict

Time: 15 minutes; *Materials:* Director's clapboard (optional); *References:* Slide #46, The $20K Conflict; Slide: #47, Questions for Understanding Needs.

- **Show Slide #46:** The $20K Conflict.

- **Say:** Next you will have an opportunity to apply the four steps to a conflict.

- **Recruit (ahead of time)** a volunteer to assist you in role playing a conflict between two parties who have been awarded $20K.

- **Agree on** the position each party will take: one wants to give the money to a charity or another worthy cause, while the other wants to spend it on travel or other personal luxuries. Have the volunteer take whichever position he or she is most comfortable portraying in the role play. Make sure the volunteer understands that the two of you will alternate playing out your conflict while allowing the participants to ask questions to uncover more information about your needs. Although the two of you will start out diametrically opposed, you should both begin to show more interest and empathy toward each other's positions as the participants are successful in uncovering your needs.

- **Explain** to participants the following conditions: you and the volunteer are business partners who have been awarded the $20K grant. You must spend the money (you cannot invest it) and you can't divide it (and so must agree on how to spend it together).

- **Instruct** the group that their job is to serve as consultants to the two of you by asking you questions to uncover your needs and interests. Forbid them to offer solutions!

- **Show Slide #47:** Questions for Understanding Needs, as a "crib sheet" for participants.

- **Role play** the conflict for a few minutes, then stop the action, using the director's clapboard (if available). Don't allow the group to get into any solutions. Have fun, with both parties being initially adamant about their positions.

- **Instruct** participants to ask you each questions to elicit your needs. *Do not allow any questions that suggest solutions to the conflict.*

- **Continue** the role play until a point is reached at which each side has a better understanding of the other's position.

- **Ask** participants what has been accomplished by the information the two parties have stated publicly.

- **Suggest,** if not stated by participants, that two things are accomplished:

  Each side understands the other better and will be more motivated to seek a win/win solution, if possible.

  The new information may hint at an actual resolution to the conflict.

- **Ask** participants to suggest possible win/win solutions to the conflict. (For example, a travel destination can include a charitable act or the tax deduction for a charitable contribution can be given to the person who wants some money for travel or another luxury.)

WORKBOOK p. 49

Conflict Worksheet

⋆✦ ✦

What is the conflict?

_____

_____

What type of conflict is it?
- ❑ Over facts or data
- ❑ Over process or methods
- ❑ Over goals or purposes
- ❑ Over values

What are the conflict styles?

Yours	Theirs
Confrontational	Confrontational
Persuasive	Persuasive
Cooperative	Cooperative
Avoiding	Avoiding

What are the positions?

Yours	Theirs
_____	_____
_____	_____
_____	_____

What are the needs of both parties?

Yours:	Theirs:
_____	_____
_____	_____
_____	_____

What are some possible solutions?

_____

_____

WORKBOOK p. 50

TRY IT: Experiments in Change

⋆✦ ✦

Select one of the following experiments. . . .

Describing a Conflict:
☐

Identify a longstanding disagreement you have been having with someone. How have you been defining the problem? See whether you can state the problem in mutual terms such as, *"The conflict we are having is . . ."* or *"Our conflict is. . . ."* Do the issues look different when you frame the conflict this way? Decide what type of conflict you are having with this person. Is it over facts, methods, purposes, or values? Are there any different approaches to the conflict you might take, based on your analysis?

Analyzing Conflict Style:
☐

Identify your own usual style of dealing with conflict. Are you primarily confrontational, persuasive, cooperative, or avoiding? List some examples of conflict situations in which you relied on this particular style. What were the consequences? Choose an alternative style you might have used in each of these situations. What would you have done differently?

Identifying Interests:
☐

Select a current or recent conflict you have been dealing with. Write down the positions taken by you and the other party. Now brainstorm your own interests in the situation, as well as those of the other party. Have these issues been addressed at all in your efforts to resolve the conflict? How might you put them on the table?

Brainstorming Solutions:
☐

Choose a current conflict situation and brainstorm as many mutual gain options as you can. Do you think any of these solutions might be workable? Consider sharing your list with the other party and inviting the person to add his or her own ideas.

Closing

Time: 10 minutes: *References:* Workbook, pp. 49–50.

- **Say:** As we wind up this module, I'd like you to work with a tool that ties together the conflict resolution elements we've been working with.

- **Refer to Workbook, p. 49:** Conflict Worksheet.

- **Instruct** them to identify a current or recent conflict they have been dealing with and to use the worksheet to analyze their conflict situation. Tell them they do not have to complete the entire worksheet in this session, but should begin and do as much as they are able to do comfortably in the next five minutes or so.

- **Call time** after five or six minutes and ask participants to discuss their ideas so far with their partners.

- **Refer to Workbook, p. 50:** TRY IT: Experiments in Change.

- **Encourage** them to select an "experiment in change" to try on the job. If there is adequate time between sessions, have them try a chosen experiment before the group reconvenes.

- **Say:** In the next module we will be turning to the skill of being a team player. It is a skill that poses challenges beyond any of the skills we have considered so far.

Being a Team Player

Suggested Time: 90 minutes.

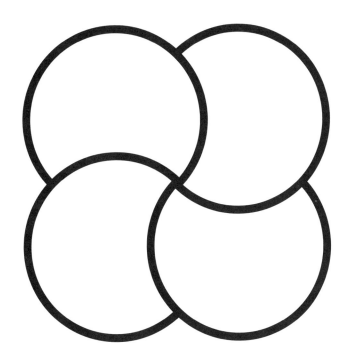

SLIDE #48: Being a Team Player

SLIDE #49: "Ask not what your teammates can do for you . . ."

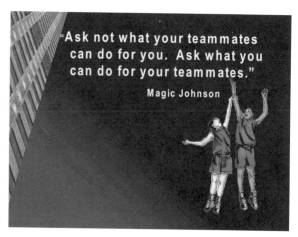

WORKBOOK p. 51

MODULE **8**

Being a Team Player

"Ask not what your teammates can do for you. Ask what you can do for your teammates."

—Magic Johnson

In this module, you will have the opportunity to . . .

- discuss the challenges of being a team player

- assess collaboration skills

- identify work situations in which collaboration is essential

- examine three ways to promote teamwork

- practice team facilitation

- select "experiments in change" at work

51

Introduction

Time: 5 minutes; *References:* Slide #48, Being a Team Player; Slide #49, "Ask not . . ."; Workbook, p. 51.

- **Show Slide #48:** Being a Team Player.

- **Say:** Being a team player is a complex skill and one that's increasingly important to all of us in today's work world.

- **Show Slide #49:** "Ask not what your teammates can do for you. . . ."

- **Say:** Here are some words of wisdom for us about being on a team. And let's look at our objectives for this module.

- **Refer to Workbook, p. 51:** Being a Team Player.

- **Review** objectives.

- **Say:** Being a member of a team really tests you because you have less personal control over the outcome than in a one-to-one relationship. It's often frustrating since you have fewer opportunities to get your point across and persuade others when participation has to be shared among many. On the other hand, being part of a team effort, even with its frustrations, can often be exciting and productive.

- **Demonstrate** this point by doing the following:

  Request a volunteer to come up to the front of the class. Hold the person's hand and spin a tale about the longstanding relationship you've had with this person. Then request another volunteer so that there is now a group of three.

  Ask the audience to imagine that you have now become a working trio for a month.

- **Say:** With [insert the name of the first volunteer], there was one relationship. How many relationships exist in our group of three?

- **When** you hear the correct answer (six), show the possibilities by having each grouping hold hands: A's relationship with B; B's relationship with C; A's relationship with C; A + B's relationship with C; B + C's relationship with A; A + C's relationship with B.

- **Ask** participants to imagine how many relationships exist in a group of six people. (The answer: 720!)

Name Tents (Optional)

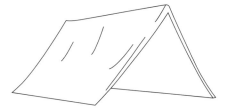

Envelopes: Broken Squares

WORKBOOK p. 52

Some Lessons from "Broken Squares"

- It's crucial to be aware of the needs (or "job") of others, as well as your own.

- Teamwork is hampered when there is little or no communication.

- You have to be patient in teams. It takes time for things to come together.

- You may figure things out individually before others. It's frustrating when you can't simply tell people what to do, but it may be necessary not to do so to give them the opportunity to do it themselves.

- Sometimes, for the good of the team, you may have to start over again.

- There is a thrill in team accomplishment.

Broken Squares

Time: 15 minutes; *Materials:* Name tents; broken squares in envelopes (see Appendix C); *References:* Workbook, p. 52.

- **Say:** With so much going on, it's critical for everyone on a team to have collaboration skills. We're about to do an exercise to dramatize how difficult that can be.

- **Divide** participants into groups of, ideally, five.

- **Tell** participants that they will be working in these groups for the remainder of the module and invite them to take a minute to come up with a name for their team. [*It may help to limit the name categories to, for instance, types of animals, cars, etc., so the task can be accomplished quickly.*] Have the teams make name tents for their groups.

- **Say:** This exercise is called "Broken Squares." You will need to pay careful attention to my instructions. The first thing you must do is clear all your books and extraneous materials from the tabletops so you will have an uncluttered work space.

- **Distribute** one set of five envelopes per team with parts of the broken squares inside.

- **Ask** each team member to take an envelope. If you have teams with fewer than five members, ask some members to take two envelopes. If there are more than five on a team, ask two members to share an envelope or invite the additional members to act as observers in the exercise.

- **Instruct** participants to empty the contents of their envelopes and observe the pieces they have.

- **Announce** that the goal of the exercise, or "the job" of each member, is to create a 6-inch square in front of him or her. Explain that, if they have two envelopes, their "job" is to create two squares, and if they are sharing an envelope, to create one square together.

- **Tell** participants they must follow these rules: No one may speak during the exercise. They may not request, verbally or nonverbally, a piece from someone else, nor take a piece from anyone. They may not dump unwanted pieces into the center of the table. They may give one or more pieces to another member at any time, but may not show the member what to do with the piece. They may not overlap the pieces or tear them apart.

- **Start** the exercise and make sure participants are obeying the rules. Recruit any observers to assist you with this.

- **Continue** playing until all five squares are made. If the groups are still struggling after five minutes, allow them to talk to each other. (What usually happens is that one or more people make a square and think that their "job" is done. However, their square will have to be dismantled and parts given to other members for all five squares to be built. The "sacrifice" and sharing that occur is the whole point of the exercise.)

- **Debrief** by asking participants to brainstorm as many points or lessons about teamwork contained in the exercise as they can.

- **Refer to Workbook, p. 52:** Some Lessons from "Broken Squares".

- **Review** the lessons listed, relating them to participants' responses.

SLIDE #50: Things Team Players Do

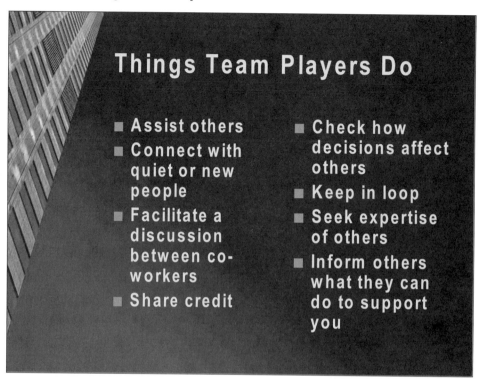

PQ
Scale

WORKBOOK p. 53

Being a Team Player   53

Things Team Players Do

⋆⋆★

Read and discuss the following list of things team players do:

1. Assist someone else when appropriate.

2. Ask quiet or new teammates for their opinions.

3. Facilitate a discussion with teammates who are in conflict.

4. Share credit you receive for a job well done.

5. Check to see how your decisions might affect others.

6. Include everyone in the information loop.

7. Seek information and expertise of others.

8. Inform others what they can do to support your efforts and ask them to tell you when they need help.

From the list, identify two actions you see as especially important in your work situation:

A. _____

B. _____

Things Team Players Do

Time: 10 minutes; *Materials:* PQ Scale; *References:* Slide #50, Things Team Players Do; Workbook, p. 53.

- **Say:** As the Broken Squares exercise demonstrated, it takes a lot to be an effective team player. Let's look at just what it may take.

- **Refer participants to PQ Scale:** PeopleSmart Skill 7.

- **Ask** them to take another look at their strengths and weaknesses.

- **Say:** Here's another list of what it takes to be a team player.

- **Show Slide #50:** Things Team Players Do.

- **Review** the list briefly.

- **Refer to Workbook, p. 53:** Things Team Players Do.

- **Instruct** participants to identify two items on the list that they feel are especially important in their own work situations.

- **Invite** them to go around the group and hear the selections of each person.

- **Say:** Now let's take the discussion of teamwork to another level.

SLIDE #51: Winter Survival

WORKBOOK p. 54

Building a Climate of Dialogue

We use the expression "everyone is entitled to his or her own opinion" when we want to support freedom of speech. However, there are social limits to this right in team situations. Too often, team discussion becomes a debate of my idea versus your idea. People advocate for the causes dear to their hearts, hoping to gain support from others. The climate becomes very politicized. By contrast, when a climate of dialogue exists, team members listen to each other, react to and build on each other's ideas, and look for and acknowledge real differences of opinion. Dialogue means "two minds together." The purpose of dialogue is to enlarge ideas, not diminish them. Here are ways you can help to build a climate of dialogue:

- Ask questions to clarify what others are saying.
- Invite others to seek clarification of your ideas.
- Share what's behind your ideas. Reveal your assumptions and goals. Invite others to do so in kind.
- Ask others to give you feedback about your ideas.
- Give constructive feedback about the ideas of others.
- Make suggestions that build on the ideas of others.
- Incorporate the ideas of others into your proposals.
- Find common ground among the ideas expressed in the group.
- Encourage others to give additional ideas from those already expressed.

Winter Survival

Time: 25 minutes; *References:* Slide #51, Winter Survival; Slide #52, Building a Climate of Dialogue; Workbook, pp. 54, 55.

- **Refer to Workbook, p. 54:** Building a Climate of Dialogue.
- **Read aloud** the opening paragraphs and ask participants to take turns reading aloud the bulleted points.
- **Say:** I want to challenge everyone to build a climate of dialogue. In the next activity, your group will face a situation in which you are likely to "die" if you don't "die-a-logue."
- **Show Slide #51:** Winter Survival.

SLIDE #52: Building a Climate of Dialogue

Building a Climate of Dialogue

- Ask questions and invite others to seek clarification.
- Reveal your assumptions and goals.
- Ask others for feedback.
- Give constructive feedback.
- Make suggestions that build on ideas.
- Incorporate others' ideas.
- Find common ground.
- Encourage additional ideas.

WORKBOOK p. 55

Being a Team Player   **55**

Winter Survival

You have just crash-landed in the woods of northern Minnesota. It is 11:32 a.m. in mid-January. The light plane in which you were traveling crashed on a lake. The pilot and copilot were killed. Shortly after the crash, the plane sank completely into the lake with the pilot's and copilot's bodies inside. None of you are seriously injured and you are all dry.

The crash came suddenly, before the pilot had time to radio for help or inform anyone of your position. Since your pilot was trying to avoid a storm, you know the plane was considerably off course. The pilot announced shortly before the crash that you were twenty miles northwest of a small town that is the nearest known habitation.

You are in a wilderness area made up of thick woods broken by many lakes and streams. The snow depth varies from above the ankles in windswept areas to knee-deep where it has drifted. The last weather report indicated that the temperature would reach minus 25 degrees Fahrenheit in the daytime and minus 40 at night. There is plenty of dead wood and twigs in the immediate area. You are dressed in winter clothing appropriate for wear in Washington, D.C. (your departure city) and Seattle (your destination).

While escaping from the plane, you were able to salvage the twelve items listed below. You may assume that the number of passengers is the same as the number of persons in your group. **Your group has agreed to stick together.**

With these resources, develop a plan for survival.

- Ball of steel wool
- Newspapers (one per person)
- Compass
- Ax
- Cigarette lighter (no fluid)
- Loaded .45 caliber pistol
- Sectional air map
- 20 × 20 foot piece of heavy-duty canvas
- Extra shirts and pants for all
- Can of shortening
- Quart of 100-proof whiskey
- Family-size chocolate bar (one per person)

- **Refer to Workbook, p. 55:** Winter Survival.

- **Read** the situation aloud.

- **Say:** Your group's job is to develop a survival plan using the resources you have salvaged. Unlike the TV show, "Survivor," where people were voted off the island, in this case *you must stick together as a group. Remember:* You will either dialogue or die.

- **Give** the group fifteen minutes to develop a survival plan.

- **Show Slide #52:** Building a Climate of Dialogue.

- **Say:** You may wish to refer to this as a "crib sheet" while discussing your survival plan.

- **Call time** after fifteen minutes. Tell the groups that before you ask them to share their survival plans, you would like them to briefly assess the quality of their dialogue.

- **Refer back to Workbook page 54:** Building a Climate of Dialogue.

- **Instruct** them to take two or three minutes to evaluate the quality of their dialogue against the bulleted items on the page.

- **Invite** the groups in turn to share their survival plans. Probe for details on how they are going to make a fire.

- **After** each of the groups has shared their plan, give each group brief feedback on their survival prospects.

- **Explain:** According to experts, you will not survive traveling to the next area of habitation. You will freeze to death, no matter what steps you take, before you reach it. In drifts as high as you will encounter, and with many trees to be circumnavigated, the trek is considerably more than the announced mileage. You must stay put. However, if you do so, your chances for rescue are surprisingly good. There will be a search party looking for you. Even the smallest planes must file a flight plan, and when your flight failed to reach its destination, a search party would be deployed. Without foliage on the trees, you should be easily visible. You can keep yourselves warm with the extra clothing and paper for insulation and by staying under the canvas. You must build a fire, both to stay warm and to provide a smoke signal (by day) and a fire signal (by night). The only reliable way to build a fire is to catch sparks from the lighter on the steel wool and then use it to ignite dry sticks and paper. After a fire starts, you have plenty of wood to keep it roaring (even wet wood will do). If there happens to be sunshine, you can get creative by applying the shortening to the lid of the can and holding it up to the sun. This will signal your presence for miles away.

- **Debrief** by pointing out that this was a fictitious situation, but in real-life team situations, the life and health of the group also depend on dialogue.

- **Say:** You are about to do some creative problem solving on a work-related issue.

Post-it Notes

Index Cards

Flip Chart: Problem Solving

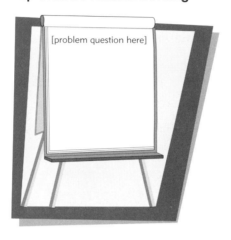

[problem question here]

WORKBOOK p. 56

56   *PeopleSmart: Participant Workbook*

Real-World Problem Solving

 ★ ✦ ★

Directions

1. Your group's task is to find solutions to the problem:

   _____

   _____

2. First, record your own "out of the box" ideas on Post-it Notes (one idea per note). Post your completed ideas on the wall.

3. Bring an index card and review the "gallery of ideas." Write down on the card ideas that seem worthwhile.

4. Using your notes from the "gallery," hold a team discussion, taking turns facilitating as directed.

Debrief

1. What will you do with your ideas?

2. What facilitation behaviors were helpful?

Real-World Problem Solving

Time: 30 minutes; *Materials:* Post-it Notes, index cards, prepared flip chart; *References:* Workbook, p. 56.

- **Refer** participants to prepared flip chart listing a real-world problem, such as: *"How can we increase employee retention? Productivity? Self-responsibility?"* (Choose one or substitute any other problem that is appropriate to the group.)

- **Say:** You are going to have an opportunity to do some "out of the box" thinking about this problem, first individually and then with your team.

- **Refer to Workbook, p. 56:** Real-World Problem Solving.

- **Instruct** them to begin by writing in the problem they are working on, from the flip chart.

- **Refer** them to Step 2. Give participants Post-it Notes and ask them to write down their own creative ideas to solve the problem, limiting themselves to one or two ideas per person, and writing only one idea per note.

- **Give** participants about three minutes to write their ideas, then call time.

- **Tell** participants to post their completed notes on a wall, creating a "gallery of ideas."

- **Refer** participants to Step 3. Give each participant an index card.

- **Tell** them to tour the gallery and write down ideas that seem worthwhile to consider.

- **Reconvene** the groups.

- **Refer** them to Step 4. Explain that they will have fifteen minutes to reach a decision about how to best deal with the problem under discussion.

- **Instruct** the teams to determine whose birthday in their group occurs first in the calendar year, and whose last. Have the two individuals in each group identify themselves, then explain that the person with the first birthday will facilitate the first half or the discussion and the person with the last birthday will facilitate the second half. Tell them you will signal them when it is time to switch.

- **Instruct** the groups to begin their discussions and signal the change in facilitators after half the time has elapsed.

- **Debrief** by inviting the groups to discuss among themselves how they may want to follow up on their ideas (for instance, by emailing their recommendations to others, sharing them with upper management, etc.).

- **Ask** participants whether any of them would like to "brag" about any helpful behaviors their facilitators used. Discuss one or two responses.

WORKBOOK p. 57

TRY IT: Experiments in Change

★★★

Select one of the following experiments. . . .

Identifying Teamwork
Opportunities:

Make a list of things you do independently of others at work. Examine the list and identify items for which it would be helpful if you involved others rather than doing things alone.

Improving Group Process:

If you are a member of a group that you would like to see improve, suggest using interactive discussion formats and creative approaches to problem solving. Identify roles that you could play to help facilitate teamwork, such as heading a subcommittee, publishing group accomplishments, or even leading a meeting.

Improving
Decision Making:

Think about how your work team makes decisions. Is it by voting? Do powerful members express their preferences and everyone else simply goes along? Talk up the advantages of reaching decisions by consensus. Listen to people's concerns about the time required and other issues. Suggest ways these concerns can be alleviated.

Incorporating Minority
Opinions:

Observe how minority opinion is dealt with in your team meetings. Are people with dissenting opinions brushed aside? Identify specific steps you can take to help the group hear from the minority.

Closing

Time: 5 minutes; *References:* Workbook, p. 57.

- **Say:** Many people dread working on teams and find them frustrating. But teams can be productive and fulfilling if members learn to "think we, not me" and operate as effective team players. I hope this module has given you some strategies for doing this.

- **Refer to Workbook, p. 57:** TRY IT: Experiments in Change.

- **Encourage** them to select an "experiment in change" to try out on the job. If there is adequate time between sessions, have them try a chosen experiment before the group reconvenes.

- **Say:** As challenging as teamwork is, many people think our next skill, shifting gears, is the hardest one of all.

Shifting Gears

Suggested Time: 60 minutes.

Banana (optional)

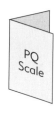

Flip Chart: "Cross Out the Letters"

SLIDE #53: Shifting Gears

WORKBOOK p. 59

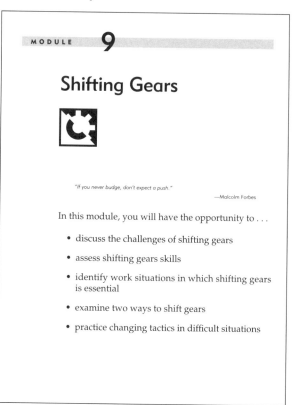

WORKBOOK p. 60

60   *PeopleSmart: Participant Workbook*

"Cross Out the Letters"

⭐⭑⭐

Directions

Cross out six letters so that the remaining letters, without altering their sequence, spell a familiar English word.

B S A I N X L E A T N T E A R S

SLIDE #54: "If you never budge, don't expect a push."

Introduction

Time: 15 minutes; *Materials:* Prepared flip chart, BSAINXLEATNTEARS; banana (optional); PQ Scale; *References:* Slide #53, Shifting Gears; Slide #54, "If you never budge. . . ."; Workbook, pp. 59, 60.

- **Show Slide #53:** Shifting Gears.
- **Say:** The final PeopleSmart skill involves shifting gears when relationships are stuck.
- **Refer to Workbook, p. 59:** Shifting Gears.
- **Review** objectives.
- **Refer** participants to prepared flip chart: Cross Out the Letters.
- **Instruct** participants as follows: In the following line of letters, cross out six letters so that the remaining letters, without altering their sequence, spell a familiar English word.
- **Refer to Workbook, p. 60:** Cross Out the Letters so they can work on the problem.
- **Expect** no one to find the solution. As participants struggle with the puzzle, you may ask whether any of them are feeling stuck and, if so, what that feels like. If someone does solve the puzzle, give the person a banana (optional).
- **Explain** (Hold up the banana, if available): You must cross out the letters that spell "six letters" and you're left with the word "banana." Demonstrate on the flip chart.
- **Say:** We began with this exercise to make the point that when we get stuck, we give up the belief that there is something else that can be done and believe that there are obstacles that permanently block the path to achieving results. The obstacles are sometimes within us. Look at this quotation.
- **Show Slide #54:** "If you never budge, don't expect a push."
- **Invite** discussion on its meaning.
- **Add** these observations to the discussion: Only you can change yourself. Finding fault with someone else doesn't change anything. Expecting someone else to change is often fruitless. When you don't budge, other people won't either. Everyone is frozen in place. If you always stay put, other people will give up on you (and themselves). We don't budge about a lot of things . . . our positions, the way we do things, our perceptions and beliefs, and so forth. While it's good to be grounded in a set of core values and actions, it is sometimes necessary to change our thinking and behaviors in specific situations.
- **Refer participants to PQ Scale:** PeopleSmart Skill 8.
- **Instruct** them to review their strengths and weaknesses on PeopleSmart Skill 8.
- **Say:** Let's take a look at two examples of shifting—or *not* shifting—gears.

Video Clip 4: Shifting Gears

WORKBOOK p. 61

Shifting Gears   61

An Example of Shifting Gears

Harry was dismayed that his suggestions were rarely taken seriously by his boss. When he evaluated the situation, he realized that, once rebuffed, he would lie low for a while, even for days at a time, before offering new ideas. Harry decided to give suggestions more frequently, even if they were rejected. Each time he was rebuffed, he graciously accepted the rejection with the comment, "Maybe my next idea will be better." This change in tactics still led nowhere, but Harry noticed that each time he made a suggestion, the boss made more of an effort to explain why it would not work for him. Next, he noticed that his boss would sometimes act on one of Harry's suggestions without saying so. Although Harry wanted credit where it was due, he nonetheless was grateful that he was starting to have an impact on his boss. It wasn't until weeks later that Harry's boss finally began thanking him for his ideas.

Two Examples

Time: 10 minutes; *References:* Video Clip #4, Shifting Gears; Workbook, p. 61.

- **Say:** The video you are about to see shows Allan and his client, Peter, in what we can safely say is a stuck relationship. Watch and decide whom you think is stuck.

- **Show Video Clip #4:** Shifting Gears.

- **Ask:** Who is stuck in this relationship? (Most participants will answer: Allan.)

- **Say:** Both are stuck. Allan keeps trying approaches he's used in the past, but Peter is also stuck because he hasn't found a way to help Allan understand what he wants. He merely berates him. A stuck relationship can be like a dance, where both parties keep doing the same steps. Either could change, but neither does.

- **Say:** In contrast, let's look at a second example of shifting gears.

- **Refer to Workbook, p. 61:** An Example of Shifting Gears.

- **Recruit** a participant to read aloud the case of "Harry."

- **Ask:** Is Harry's story a successful example of shifting gears? In what way?

- **Discuss responses.** Point out, as necessary, that Harry takes responsibility for changing his own behavior, even though his boss may not be treating him fairly, and that Harry is persistent and doesn't give up in the face of initial disappointments.

- **Say:** Let's turn to our own real-life situations and talk about how to follow Harry's example.

- **Instruct** participants to rotate to new partners.

SLIDE #55: How to Shift Gears   **SLIDE #56: Assess the Relationship**

How to Shift Gears

- Figure out what's stuck
- Act in novel ways

Assess the Relationship

- Evaluate emotional closeness
- Look for style differences
- Notice repetitive cycles of behavior

WORKBOOK p. 62

---

62   *PeopleSmart: Participant Workbook*

Getting Unstuck

★ ★ ★

Directions

1. Identify a relationship in which you feel a need to get unstuck:

    _____ Your boss

    _____ One of your customers

    _____ One of your direct reports

    _____ One of your teammates or coworkers

2. Figure out what's stuck in this situation. Evaluate the dynamics of the relationship. Ask yourself questions such as:

    • Am I too enmeshed with this person? Do I need to back off and give him/her more space?

    • Are we too disengaged? Do I need to communicate more often with this person or give him/her more support?

    Analyze differences in style between you and the other person. Consider:

    • Do we have different styles? To what extent is each of us inclined to be . . .

        concerned with facts and logic

        friendly and empathic

        comfortable taking charge

        enthusiastic and impulsive

    Assess how your interactions with this person typically go.

    • What behaviors do each of you keep repeating nearly every time you are stuck on something?

    The other person's behavior: _____

    _____

    _____

    Your response: _____

    _____

Getting Unstuck

Time: 20 minutes; *References:* Slide #55, How to Shift Gears; Slide #56, Assess the Relationship; Workbook, p. 62.

- **Say:** Sometimes all of us are more like Allan than Harry. Let me give an example from my own experience.

- **Tell** participants briefly about a stuck relationship from your own experience in which you were unsuccessful at shifting gears. Invite them to help you analyze your stuck relationship.

- **Show Slide #55:** How to Shift Gears.

- **Say:** If I wanted to shift gears in my situation, all I would need to do is two things: figure out what's stuck and act in a new way. Of course, we all know that's easier said than done. But let's talk through the first step to see how I might get a better handle on how I'm stuck.

- **Show Slide #56:** Assess the Relationship.

- **Say**: One thing I can consider is to evaluate the emotional closeness or distance between myself and the other person. If we are too close, we're like two fingers caught in a Chinese handcuff. Every action one takes intrudes on and limits the other. You don't feel that you have your own space. If we are too distant, we're like two ships passing in the night. We have little involvement in each other's lives. Important information about the other person is usually not divulged. Each party goes about his or her own business.

- **Ask**: How would you assess what's going in my relationship? Do you think it is too close or too distant?

- **Discuss** responses.

- **Say**: Another thing I can do is to look for style differences. Remember that we touched on this in the "Understanding People" module. Perhaps my counterpart and I have very different ways of viewing and acting in the world. Maybe our styles clash. What do you think? Is one of us easygoing and the other more intense? Is one of us more of a talker and the other more of a doer? How might our styles be different?

- **Discuss** responses.

- **Say**: Finally, I can try to notice repetitive cycles of behavior. Imagine someone watching the two of us on videotape. Regardless of what scene is being played, do you think the viewer would see basically the same "dance" between us?

- **Discuss** responses.

- **Say:** Now it's your turn to look at a stuck relationship of your own.

- **Refer to Workbook, p. 62:** Getting Unstuck.

- **Instruct** participants to identify a work relationship in which they feel a need to shift gears, referring to the list on the top of the page.

- **Invite** them to assess the relationship with their partner, using the steps on Workbook page 62 to figure out what's stuck. [*If time is limited, do one round only.*]

- **Debrief** by asking one or two volunteers to share any insights they gained from the exercise.

SLIDE #57: How to Shift Gears

WORKBOOK p. 63 (Continued)

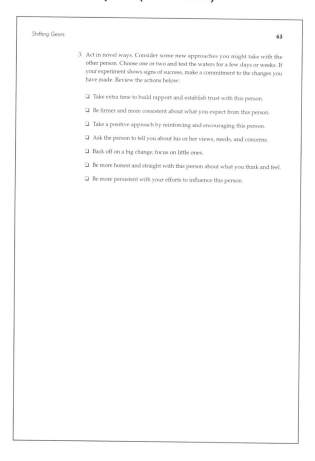

Shifting Gears   63

3. Act in novel ways. Consider some new approaches you might take with the other person. Choose one or two and test the waters for a few days or weeks. If your experiment shows signs of success, make a commitment to the changes you have made. Review the actions below:

❑ Take extra time to build rapport and establish trust with this person.

❑ Be firmer and more consistent about what you expect from this person.

❑ Take a positive approach by reinforcing and encouraging this person.

❑ Ask the person to tell you about his or her views, needs, and concerns.

❑ Back off on a big change; focus on little ones.

❑ Be more honest and straight with this person about what you think and feel.

❑ Be more persistent with your efforts to influence this person.

A New Approach

Time: 15 minutes; *References:* Slide #57, How to Shift Gears; Workbook, p. 63.

- **Show Slide #57:** How to Shift Gears.

- **Say:** Once you've considered what might be stuck in a relationship, it's time to take the next step and change tactics.

- **Refer to Workbook, p. 63:** Getting Unstuck (continued).

- **Invite** them to look over the list of novel actions.

- **Ask:** Do you think any of these might be helpful for me to try in my relationship?

- **Discuss** responses.

- **Instruct** participants to discuss the list with their partners and choose a possible new approach for their own stuck relationship. [*If time is short, do just one round, referring to the relationship discussed in the previous exercise.*]

- **Debrief** by returning to the volunteers from the previous exercise to see if they found a promising new approach.

- **Summarize:** Shifting gears is perhaps the most difficult skill involved in being people smart, but when we can do it, new opportunities open to us. This module does not include experiments in change because shifting gears *is* an experiment in change.

- **Say:** The last module will help you prepare to carry the people smart skills forward into your day-to-day work situations.

PeopleSmart Day-by-Day

Suggested Time: 60 minutes.

PROP: *$1,000,000* bills (optional)

Flip Chart: Contestant Winnings

WORKBOOK p. 65

MODULE **10**

PeopleSmart Day-by-Day

"It does not matter how slowly you go, so long as you do not stop."
—Confucius

In this module, you will have the opportunity to . . .

- review the eight skills
- develop an action plan for the next month
- arrange with a partner for follow-up
- reflect on what you've learned

65

SLIDE #58: PeopleSmart Day-by-Day

SLIDE #59: Who Wants to Be a Millionaire?

Reviewing Working PeopleSmart

Time: 25 minutes; *Materials:* $1,000,000 bills (optional); flip chart to tally "contestants'" winnings; *References:* Slide #58, PeopleSmart Day-by-Day; Slide #59, Who Wants to Be a Millionaire?; Workbook, pp. 65, 66–68.

- **Show Slide #58:** PeopleSmart Day-by-Day.
- **Refer to Workbook, p. 65:** PeopleSmart Day-by-Day.
- **Review** objectives.
- **Show Slide #59:** Who Wants to Be a Millionaire?
- **Say:** Once again, we are going to use a modified version of "Who Wants to Be a Millionaire?"—this time to review the contents of the course in a fun way.
- **Pair** participants with a new partner. Each pair will act as a single contestant. Alternatively, return participants to their teams from Module 8.

WORKBOOK p. 66

Reviewing Working PeopleSmart

★★★

$100

The first PeopleSmart skill is
- ❏ Avoiding trouble
- ❏ Exchanging feedback
- ❏ Understanding people
- ❏ Letting it all hang out

$200

Resolving conflict effectively involves
- ❏ Win/lose solutions
- ❏ Lose/lose solutions
- ❏ Win/win solutions
- ❏ Arguing

$500

Being a team player does not involve
- ❏ Patience
- ❏ Collaboration
- ❏ Sharing the credit
- ❏ Constant fun

$1,000

Besides giving feedback to others, it's important to
- ❏ Ask them for money
- ❏ Let them know they are helpless
- ❏ Leave as soon as possible
- ❏ Ask them for feedback about yourself

WORKBOOK p. 67

$2,000

The best way to assert yourself is to
- ❏ Be loud
- ❏ Remain calm and confident
- ❏ Apologize first
- ❏ Justify your actions

$4,000

A good way to understand others is
- ❏ To give them psychological tests
- ❏ To look at how you compare to them
- ❏ To give them feedback
- ❏ To trust your gut

$8,000

The percentage of people fired for poor interpersonal skills is
- ❏ 60 percent
- ❏ 98 percent
- ❏ 76 percent
- ❏ 90 percent

$16,000

To shift gears, it may be helpful to
- ❏ Try a new approach, even when you're in the right
- ❏ Examine who started you off in the wrong direction
- ❏ Use trial and error
- ❏ Take a vacation

$32,000

Which is not a good way to include the listener?
- ❏ Feed information in chunks
- ❏ Repeat yourself like a broken record
- ❏ Give the big picture first
- ❏ Share the microphone

WORKBOOK p. 68

$64,000

The seven intelligences do not include
- ❏ Introspection
- ❏ Visual acuity
- ❏ Logical reasoning
- ❏ People smarts

$250,000

The best thing to do if you have a strong need to give advice is to
- ❏ Slow yourself down
- ❏ Drop your agenda for a while
- ❏ Manage your emotions
- ❏ Make your points more compelling

$500,000

Who was *not* quoted in this course?
- ❏ Marion Anderson
- ❏ Patricia Jakubowski
- ❏ Yogi Berra
- ❏ Steven Forbes

$1,000,000

The most consistently important PeopleSmart behavior is to
- ❏ Go through the front door instead of the back door
- ❏ Ask questions
- ❏ Tell others what's in it for them
- ❏ Give a sincere rationale

- **Refer to Workbook, pp. 66–68:** Reviewing Working PeopleSmart.

- **Instruct** participants to answer the multiple-choice review questions as a pair (or team). Tell them to choose the best of the available answers for each question and *not* to look up the correct answers in their workbooks. Allow time for them to answer the questions.

- **Assign** a number to each pair or, if working with teams, assign or draw numbers to determine the order in which "contestants" will respond to the questions.

- **Set up** a flip chart to tally the "winnings" of each pair or team.

- **Begin** with pair #1 and ask them the $100 question. Then turn to pair #2 to answer the $200 question correctly. If one pair or team answers a question incorrectly, allow the next "contestant" a chance to respond. (You may want to allow all the contestants to give their answers to the final $1,000,000 question.)

- **Give** $1,000,000 bills, if available, to the winning pair or team.

Answers: understanding people; win/win solutions; constant fun; ask them for feedback about yourself; remain calm and confident; to look at how you compare to them; 90 percent; try a new approach, even when you're in the right; repeat yourself like a broken record; visual acuity; drop your agenda for a while; Steven Forbes; ask questions.

Index Cards

SLIDE #60: Your Personal Action Plan

WORKBOOK p. 69

PeopleSmart Day-by-Day   69

A Checklist of PeopleSmart Actions

★ ★ ★

Look over the list below and select one action from each category that is the most important for you to take.

TO UNDERSTAND PEOPLE BETTER . . .
- ❏ ask more questions
- ❏ avoid labeling
- ❏ look beyond surface behavior
- ❏ evaluate how I compare to another person (style, gender, age, culture)

TO EXPRESS MYSELF MORE CLEARLY . . .
- ❏ think before I talk
- ❏ provide more/less detail
- ❏ "give up the microphone"
- ❏ be straightforward and direct

TO ASSERT MY NEEDS BETTER . . .
- ❏ get clearer about what I want
- ❏ say no when I must
- ❏ speak up and ask for what I need
- ❏ remain calm and confident under fire

TO EXCHANGE FEEDBACK BETTER . . .
- ❏ invite others to give me feedback
- ❏ listen to the feedback others give me
- ❏ don't withhold feedback I can give
- ❏ offer suggestions instead of criticism

TO BECOME MORE INFLUENTIAL . . .
- ❏ temporarily drop my agenda and connect
- ❏ find out more about the opinions of others
- ❏ explain the benefits others may obtain
- ❏ give people time to mull over my advice

WORKBOOK p. 70

70   *PeopleSmart: Participant Workbook*

TO RESOLVE CONFLICTS MORE EFFECTIVELY . . .
- ❏ bring concerns out into the open sooner
- ❏ find out what the other party needs
- ❏ seek solutions, not victory
- ❏ persevere despite initial negative reactions

TO BECOME A BETTER COLLABORATOR . . .
- ❏ find out what teammates need
- ❏ express appreciation
- ❏ use the talents of others
- ❏ keep others informed about my activity

TO SHIFT GEARS, WHEN NECESSARY . . .
- ❏ accept when a relationship is in a rut
- ❏ look for the patterns we fall into
- ❏ take the initiative in shifting gears
- ❏ do something different

Your Personal Action Plan

Time: 20 minutes: *Materials:* Colored index cards; *References:* Slide #60, Your Personal Action Plan; Workbook, pp. 69–70.

- **Show Slide #60:** Your Personal Action Plan.

- **Say:** It's time to think about how you want to apply the PeopleSmart skills to your work world.

- **Refer to Workbook, pp. 69–70:** A Checklist of PeopleSmart Actions.

- **Instruct** them to review the suggested action steps for each of the eight skills and to choose one action for each skill that they would like to focus on applying on the job.

- **Ask** participants to select the top two actions, from the eight they identified, that they want to address within the next month.

- **Give** participants two brightly colored index cards and ask them to record on each card the top two actions they selected. Have them label one card: *My Goals* and the other card [*Fill in their name*]*'s Goals.* Explain that the card with their name on it should also have their telephone number and/or email address on the back.

- **Instruct** participants to give the card with their name and contact information to a partner and then schedule a telephone or email contact with their partners within the next month to check on each other's progress.

Ball of Yarn

The Web of Connection

Time: 15 minutes; *Materials:* Ball of yarn.

- **Say:** I would like you all to come to the front (or back) of the room for a closing group activity. (There should be room for participants to stand in a circle, facing each other. They will be using the ball of yarn to literally connect with each other.)

- **Instruct** everybody to stand and form a circle. Start the process by stating briefly what you have experienced as a result of facilitating the training program.

- **Holding** onto the end of the yarn, toss the ball to a participant on the other side of the circle. Ask that person to state briefly one of his or her goals from the previous activity. When he or she is finished, he or she is to toss the ball to another participant, while holding onto a piece.

- **Have** each participant take a turn at receiving the yarn, sharing reflections, and tossing on the yarn, continuing to hold onto a piece. The resulting visual is a web of yarn connecting every member of the group.

- **Complete** the activity by saying: This program began as a collection of individuals willing to connect and learn from each other. Now the links are real. In a people smart organization, those links can be a source of support and strength.

- **Cut** the yarn with scissors so that each person retains the piece he or she is holding.

- **Say:** We are leaving as we came, as individuals, but we are taking a piece of each other with us. Thank you all for your interest, ideas, time, and effort.

Creating a Sample "Butterfly"

MAKE THE BUTTERFLY from the same type of 8.5 by 11-inch paper you will distribute to participants.

Holding the paper vertically, fold it in half, downwards, and tear off the upper-right-hand corner. Next, fold the paper again toward your right, so that the top corner aligns with the torn corner. Tear off the overlapping corner. Fold the paper downward so that the bottom right corner aligns with the two previously torn corners. Tear off the overlapping piece, so that you are holding a folded paper with the bottom-right-hand corner completely torn off. When you unfold the paper, you will have a butterfly.

The trick to making the butterfly is to tear off (initially) the upper-right-hand corner and then rotate that paper so that each subsequent tear occurs in the same corner as the previous tear. Also, your first fold will be from top to bottom, not from side to side, as some participants will do. The completed butterfly has the shape shown below.

Be sure to prepare your butterfly ahead of time so that participants cannot watch you do it.

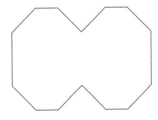

Drawings A and B in Folders

USING THE DRAWINGS on the following pages (or any rather complicated abstract shapes), reproduce enough copies of each for the number of pairs of participants in your class (e.g., six copies of each drawing for a class of twelve).

Staple each drawing into a standard file folder so that the drawing appears, face up, when the folder is open and cannot be seen when the folder is closed. Insert a blank piece of paper into each folder.

Label all folders containing the first drawing "A" and those containing the second drawing "B" (or use color-coded labels to differentiate the two sets).

Keep the "A" and "B" sets grouped separately for easy distribution to participants.

Suggestion: prior to each class, be sure to check the folders and insert new blank sheets where needed.

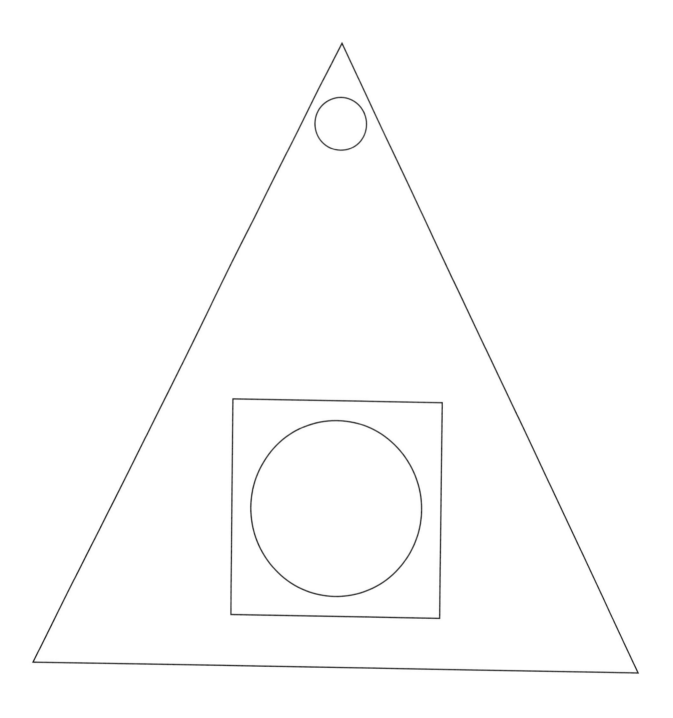

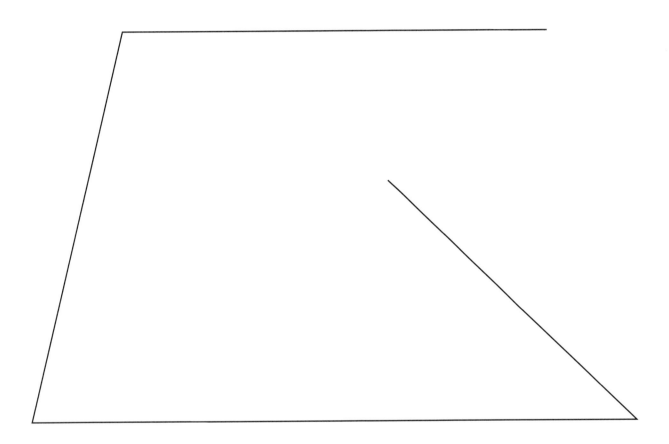

Broken Squares*

IN ADVANCE OF THE SESSION, prepare the necessary materials for this exercise as described below:

- You will be preparing a set of materials for each team. A *set consists of five envelopes* containing pieces of cardboard cut into different patterns that, when properly arranged, will form five cardboard squares of equal size.

- To prepare a set, cut out five cardboard squares, each exactly 6 inches by 6 inches. Place the squares in a row and mark them as below, penciling the numbers lightly so they can be erased.

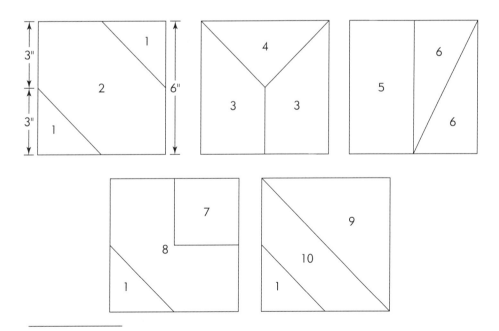

*Adapted with permission from Alex Bavelas, Communication patterns in task-oriented groups, *Journal of the Acoustical Society of America, 22,* 225–230, Copyright 1950, Acoustical Society of America.

- The lines should be drawn so that when the pieces are cut out, those marked "1" will be exactly the same size, those marked "3" the same size, and so forth. Several combinations are possible that will form one or two squares, but only one combination will form all five squares, each 6 inches by 6 inches. After drawing the lines on the squares and labeling the sections with numbers, cut each square along the lines into smaller pieces to make the parts of the puzzle.

- Label the five envelopes A, B, C, D, and E. Distribute the cardboard pieces into the five envelopes as follows: envelope A has pieces 5, 8, 9; B has 1, 1, 1, 3; C has 1, 10; D has 4, 6; and E has 2, 3, 6, 7.

- Erase the penciled numbers from each piece and write, instead, the letter of the envelope it is in. This makes it easy to return the pieces to the proper envelopes for subsequent use.

- Each *set* may be made from a different color of cardboard.

MEL SILBERMAN and FREDA HANSBURG are the authors of *PeopleSmart: Developing Your Interpersonal Intelligence* (Berrett-Koehler, 2000), *Working PeopleSmart: 6 Strategies for Success* (Berrett-Koehler, 2004), and *The 60-Minute Active Training Series* (Pfeiffer, 2005). They are also the founders of PeopleSmart Products and Services, an Active Training Company (www.activetraining. com and 800–924–8157).

Mel Silberman is known internationally as a pioneer in the areas of interpersonal skills training, active learning, and team facilitation. As a professor of adult and organizational development at Temple University, Mel won two awards for his distinguished teaching. Among his numerous publications are

Active Training, 2nd ed. (Pfeiffer, 1998)

The Best of Active Training (Pfeiffer, 2004)

101 Ways to Make Training Active, 2nd ed. (Pfeiffer, 2005)

He is also editor of *The ASTD Training and Performance Sourcebook* and *The ASTD Leadership and Organization Development Sourcebook.*

Freda Hansburg is a psychologist in private practice, a training consultant, and an executive coach whose recent clients include BMW of North America, Depository Trust and Clearing Corporation, Merck, and Valero Refining. She has contributed to *The Training and Performance Sourcebook* and has made presentations about interpersonal intelligence for ASTD and the OD Network. Freda is the former director of the Technical Assistance Center, a behavioral health consultation and training program at the University of Medicine and Dentistry of New Jersey.

System Requirements

PC with Microsoft Windows 98SE or later
Mac with Apple OS version 8.6 or later

Using the CD With Windows

To view the items located on the CD, follow these steps:

1. Insert the CD into your computer's CD-ROM drive.

2. A window appears with the following options:

    Contents: Allows you to view the files included on the CD-ROM.

    Software: Allows you to install useful software from the CD-ROM.

    Links: Displays a hyperlinked page of websites.

    Author: Displays a page with information about the Author(s).

    Contact Us: Displays a page with information on contacting the publisher or author.

    Help: Displays a page with information on using the CD.

    Exit: Closes the interface window.

If you do not have autorun enabled, or if the autorun window does not appear, follow these steps to access the CD:

1. Click Start-Run.

2. In the dialog box that appears, type d: start.exe, where d is the letter of your CD-ROM drive. This brings up the autorun window described in the preceding set of steps.

3. Choose the desired option from the menu. (See Step 2 in the preceding list for a description of these options.)

In Case of Trouble

If you experience difficulty using the CD-ROM, please follow these steps:

1. Make sure your hardware and systems configurations conform to the systems requirements noted under "System Requirements" above.

2. Review the installation procedure for your type of hardware and operating system.

It is possible to reinstall the software if necessary. To speak with someone in Product Technical Support, call 800–762–2974 or 317–572–3994 M–F 8:30 A.M.–5:00 P.M. EST. You can also get support and contact Product Technical Support through our website at www.wiley.com/techsupport.

Before calling or writing, please have the following information available:

- Type of computer and operating system
- Any error messages displayed
- Complete description of the problem.

It is best if you are sitting at your computer when making the call.

Pfeiffer Publications Guide

This guide is designed to familiarize you with the various types of Pfeiffer publications. The formats section describes the various types of products that we publish; the methodologies section describes the many different ways that content might be provided within a product. We also provide a list of the topic areas in which we publish.

FORMATS

In addition to its extensive book-publishing program, Pfeiffer offers content in an array of formats, from fieldbooks for the practitioner to complete, ready-to-use training packages that support group learning.

FIELDBOOK Designed to provide information and guidance to practitioners in the midst of action. Most fieldbooks are companions to another, sometimes earlier, work, from which its ideas are derived; the fieldbook makes practical what was theoretical in the original text. Fieldbooks can certainly be read from cover to cover. More likely, though, you'll find yourself bouncing around following a particular theme, or dipping in as the mood, and the situation, dictates.

HANDBOOK A contributed volume of work on a single topic, comprising an eclectic mix of ideas, case studies, and best practices sourced by practitioners and experts in the field.

An editor or team of editors usually is appointed to seek out contributors and to evaluate content for relevance to the topic. Think of a handbook not as a ready-to-eat meal, but as a cookbook of ingredients that enables you to create the most fitting experience for the occasion.

RESOURCE Materials designed to support group learning. They come in many forms: a complete, ready-to-use exercise (such as a game); a comprehensive resource on one topic (such as conflict management) containing a variety of methods and approaches; or a collection of like-minded activities (such as icebreakers) on multiple subjects and situations.

TRAINING PACKAGE An entire, ready-to-use learning program that focuses on a particular topic or skill. All packages comprise a guide for the facilitator/trainer and a workbook for the participants. Some packages are supported with additional media—such as video—or learning aids, instruments, or other devices to help participants understand concepts or practice and develop skills.

- *Facilitator/trainer's guide* Contains an introduction to the program, advice on how to organize and facilitate the learning event, and step-by-step instructor notes. The guide also contains copies of presentation materials—handouts, presentations, and overhead designs, for example—used in the program.
- *Participant's workbook* Contains exercises and reading materials that support the learning goal and serves as a valuable reference and support guide for participants in the weeks and months that follow the learning event. Typically, each participant will require his or her own workbook.

ELECTRONIC CD-ROMs and web-based products transform static Pfeiffer content into dynamic, interactive experiences. Designed to take advantage of the searchability, automation, and ease-of-use that technology provides, our e-products bring convenience and immediate accessibility to your workspace.

METHODOLOGIES

CASE STUDY A presentation, in narrative form, of an actual event that has occurred inside an organization. Case studies are not prescriptive, nor are they used to prove a point; they are designed to develop critical analysis and decision-making skills. A case study has a specific time frame, specifies a sequence of events, is narrative in structure, and contains a plot structure—an issue (what should be/have been done?). Use case studies when the goal is to enable participants to apply previously learned theories to the circumstances in the case, decide what is pertinent, identify the real issues, decide what should have been done, and develop a plan of action.

ENERGIZER A short activity that develops readiness for the next session or learning event. Energizers are most commonly used after a break or lunch to stimulate or refocus the group. Many involve some form of physical activity, so they are a useful way to counter post-lunch lethargy. Other uses include transitioning from one topic to another, where "mental" distancing is important.

EXPERIENTIAL LEARNING ACTIVITY (ELA) A facilitator-led intervention that moves participants through the learning cycle from experience to application (also known as a Structured Experience). ELAs are carefully thought-out designs in which there is a definite learning purpose and intended outcome. Each step—everything that participants do during the activity—facilitates the accomplishment of the stated goal. Each ELA includes complete instructions for facilitating the intervention and a clear statement of goals, suggested group size and timing, materials required, an explanation of the process, and, where appropriate, possible variations to the activity. (For more detail on Experiential Learning Activities, see the Introduction to the *Reference Guide to Handbooks and Annuals*, 1999 edition, Pfeiffer, San Francisco.)

GAME A group activity that has the purpose of fostering team sprit and togetherness in addition to the achievement of a pre-stated goal. Usually contrived—undertaking a desert expedition, for example—this type of learning method offers an engaging means for participants to demonstrate and practice business and interpersonal skills. Games are effective for team-building and personal development mainly because the goal is subordinate to the process—the means through which participants reach decisions, collaborate, communicate, and generate trust and understanding. Games often engage teams in "friendly" competition.

ICEBREAKER A (usually) short activity designed to help participants overcome initial anxiety in a training session and/or to acquaint the participants with one another. An icebreaker can be a fun activity or can be tied to specific topics or training goals. While a useful tool in itself, the icebreaker comes into its own in situations where tension or resistance exists within a group.

INSTRUMENT A device used to assess, appraise, evaluate, describe, classify, and summarize various aspects of human behavior. The term used to describe an instrument depends primarily on its format and purpose. These terms include survey, questionnaire, inventory, diagnostic, survey, and poll. Some uses of instruments include providing instrumental feedback to group members, studying here-and-now processes or functioning within a group, manipulating group composition, and evaluating outcomes of training and other interventions.

Instruments are popular in the training and HR field because, in general, more growth can occur if an individual is provided with a method for focusing specifically on his or her own behavior. Instruments also are used to obtain information that will serve as a basis for change and to assist in workforce planning efforts.

Paper-and-pencil tests still dominate the instrument landscape with a typical package comprising a facilitator's guide, which offers advice on administering the instrument and interpreting the collected data, and an initial set of instruments. Additional instruments are available separately. Pfeiffer, though, is investing heavily in e-instruments. Electronic instrumentation provides effortless distribution and, for larger groups particularly, offers advantages over paper-and-pencil tests in the time it takes to analyze data and provide feedback.

LECTURETTE A short talk that provides an explanation of a principle, model, or process that is pertinent to the participants' current learning needs. A lecturette is intended to establish a common language bond between the trainer and the participants by providing a mutual frame of reference. Use a lecturette as an introduction to a group activity or event, as an interjection during an event, or as a handout.

MODEL A graphic depiction of a system or process and the relationship among its elements. Models provide a frame of reference and something more tangible, and more easily remembered, than a verbal explanation. They also give participants something to "go on," enabling them to track their own progress as they experience the dynamics, processes, and relationships being depicted in the model.

ROLE PLAY A technique in which people assume a role in a situation/scenario: a customer service rep in an angry-customer exchange, for example. The way in which the role is approached is then discussed and feedback is offered. The role play is often repeated using a different approach and/or incorporating changes made based on feedback received. In other words, role playing is a spontaneous interaction involving realistic behavior under artificial (and safe) conditions.

SIMULATION A methodology for understanding the interrelationships among components of a system or process. Simulations differ from games in that they test or use a model that depicts or mirrors some aspect of reality in form, if not necessarily in content. Learning occurs by studying the effects of change on one or more factors of the model. Simulations are commonly used to test hypotheses about what happens in a system—often referred to as "what if?" analysis—or to examine best-case/worst-case scenarios.

THEORY A presentation of an idea from a conjectural perspective. Theories are useful because they encourage us to examine behavior and phenomena through a different lens.

TOPICS

The twin goals of providing effective and practical solutions for workforce training and organization development and meeting the educational needs of training and human resource professionals shape Pfeiffer's publishing program. Core topics include the following:

Leadership & Management

Communication & Presentation

Coaching & Mentoring

Training & Development

E-Learning

Teams & Collaboration

OD & Strategic Planning

Human Resources

Consulting

What will you find on pfeiffer.com?

- The best in workplace performance solutions for training and HR professionals

- Downloadable training tools, exercises, and content

- Web-exclusive offers

- Training tips, articles, and news

- Seamless on-line ordering

- Author guidelines, information on becoming a Pfeiffer Affiliate, and much more

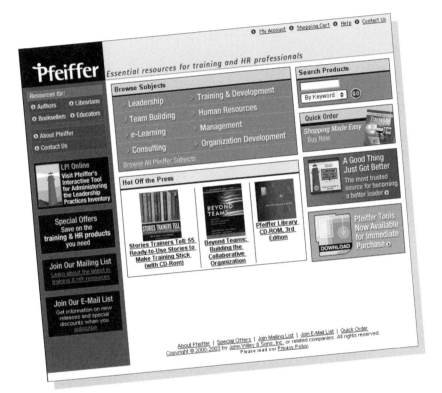

Discover more at www.pfeiffer.com

Notes